SIEGE BATTERY 94

DURING THE WORLD WAR
1914–1918

MAJOR CHARLES E. BERKELEY LOWE,
D.S.O., M.C., R.G.A.

The Naval & Military Press Ltd

published in association with

FIREPOWER
The Royal Artillery Museum
Woolwich

Published by
The Naval & Military Press Ltd
Unit 10 Ridgewood Industrial Park,
Uckfield, East Sussex,
TN22 5QE England
Tel: +44 (0) 1825 749494
Fax: +44 (0) 1825 765701
www.naval-military-press.com

in association with

FIREPOWER
The Royal Artillery Museum, Woolwich
www.firepower.org.uk

*In reprinting in facsimile from the original, any imperfections are inevitably reproduced
and the quality may fall short of modern type and cartographic standards.*

CONVENTIONAL SIGN AS SUGGESTED BY
2ND LIEUT. A. F. BISCOE, R.A.S.C.

Painted in colours as a distinguishing mark on all
Battery transport.   The shield also contains the
signs of the remaining batteries of the 23rd
Brigade R.G.A.

The Hon. Sec. 94th Siege Battery Old Comrades Association has the pleasure to send you herewith, gratis, one copy of the History of the Battery. kindly acknowledge receipt on attached form. There are about 200 copies available for sale should you wish any more copies, please fill in form below and return at once with remittance (6/6 post free per copy) orders will be executed in strict rotation.

E. HOPKINS, Esq., Brookside, Moss Lane, Pinner.
I acknowledge receipt of the History of 94th Siege Battery. I request you to send me...............................further copies for which I enclose

Yours Truly,

B.L. 9·2-inch Howitzer (Mark I.) in Firing Position.

This photograph is taken from the official handbook of the gun, and reproduced by the special and courteous permission of the Controller of His Majesty's Stationery Office.

SIEGE BATTERY 94

DURING THE WORLD-WAR 1914—1918.

COMPILED BY

MAJOR CHARLES E. BERKELEY LOWE, D.S.O., M.C., R.G.A.,

WITH AN INTRODUCTION BY

LIEUT.-COLONEL D. A. SANDFORD, D.S.O., R.G.A.

LONDON
T. WERNER LAURIE LTD.
30 NEW BRIDGE STREET, E.C. 4.

DEDICATED

TO

THE GLORIOUS MEMORY

OF

ALL RANKS OF 94 SIEGE BATTERY,

R.G.A.,

WHO, DURING THE WORLD-WAR,

1914–1918,

GAVE THEIR LIVES FOR KING AND COUNTRY.

"HERE WAS A ROYAL FELLOWSHIP OF DEATH."

CONTENTS

PAGE

INTRODUCTION - - - - - - - - 11

CHAP.

I.—FORMATION - - - - - - - - 15
   (*December, 1915—May, 1916*)

II.—THE BATTLES OF THE SOMME - - - - 17
   (*June, 1916—March, 1917*)

III.—SUBSEQUENT GERMAN RETREAT TO THE HINDEN-
   BURG LINE AND BATTLE OF ARRAS - - - 32
   (*March—May, 1917*)

IV.—THE BATTLE OF MESSINES - - - - - 36
   (*June, 1917*)

V.—OPERATIONS ON THE FLANDERS COAST - - - 43
   (*June—December, 1917*)

VI.—YPRES AND THE WINTER OF 1917–18 - - - 51
   (*December, 1917—March, 1918*)

VII.—MARCH 21ST, 1918, AND SUBSEQUENT BRITISH
   RETREAT - - - - - - - - 55
   (*March—April, 1918*)

VIII.—THE PERIOD OF RECOVERY AND RESUMPTION OF
   BRITISH OFFENSIVE - - - - - - 66
   (*May—August, 1918*)

Contents

		PAGE
IX.—THE GREAT ADVANCE	- - - - - -	72
(September—November, 1918)		
X.—DEMOBILISATION	- - - - - -	85
(November, 1918—*June,* 1919)		
XI.—(1) ROLL OF HONOUR	- - - - -	89
(2) NOMINAL ROLLS IN SIX PARTS	- - -	94
(3) SUMMARY OF BATTERY POSITIONS OCCUPIED	-	154

ILLUSTRATIONS

THE 9·2-INCH B.L. HOWITZER (MARK I.). FIRING POSITION
Frontispiece

To face page

ORIGINAL PERSONNEL OF 94 SIEGE BATTERY -   -   - 16

THORNYCROFT " J " TYPE 3½-TON, 30–35 H.P. LORRY   - 32

HOLT 75 H.P. CATERPILLAR TRACTOR   -   -   -   - 40

THE 9·2-INCH B.L. HOWITZER (MARK I.). REAR VIEW   - 48

CAPTURED GERMAN 77-MM. GUN   -   -   -   -   - 64

SNAPSHOT OF NO. 4 GUN IN ACTION AT RONSSOY   -   - 80

COPY OF ORIGINAL TELEGRAM ORDERING CESSATION OF
HOSTILITIES -   -   -   -   -   -   -   - 85

MAP OF BATTLE ZONE ON BRITISH FRONT SHOWING POSI-
TIONS OCCUPIED BY THE BATTERY, JUNE, 1916—
NOVEMBER, 1918 (SPECIALLY PREPARED BY THE
ORDNANCE SURVEY)   -   -   -   -   -   - 160

INTRODUCTION

Shortly after the Armistice it was decided to create a "94 Siege Battery Old Comrades Association" as a means of maintaining touch between past members of the Battery, and of keeping alive its spirit.

The basis of the scheme was to be a book, which should contain a Nominal Roll of all ranks who served in the Battery, and a history of its life from formation to disembodiment.

This book, thanks to the perseverance and energy of Maj. C. E. B. Lowe, D.S.O., M.C., who collected and compiled the various records, is now completed, and I have been asked to write a short " Introduction " to it, explaining the objects of our Old Comrades Association.

The writing of the history was undertaken by Maj. C. E. B. Lowe, Capt. M. S. Lush, M.C., and Capt. R. A. E. Somerville, M.C., M.M., and I am sure all my old comrades will agree with me that they have carried out their task in a most efficient and successful manner, and that we owe them a special debt of gratitude.

Speaking for myself, as I read what they had written, I lived once more in the mud and desolation of the Somme. I watched again, from our position opposite Messines, the batteries round us, which, less fortunate than ourselves, were getting " shot up," while their ammunition was blowing up with awesome detonations that made one's blood run cold. I thought anew on that grim test of endurance during six long months at

Introduction

Nieuport, where our casualties were never higher, and our shooting never better. I thrilled again with pride at thought of the men who, in March, 1918, not only saved their guns from the forefront of our broken line, but, refusing to understand that 9·2's were not field guns, turned them again and again on the enemy along that never-to-be-forgotten road back to Amiens. Best of all, as I read, I felt all around me that spirit of fellowship which made of the Battery that " happy band of brothers " which it was so great a privilege to command.

* * * *

This book will remind us of old friends, old scenes—and if, as is natural, the stirring up of old memories gives us the impulse to write to an old chum, we shall find his address ready to hand.

An Honorary Secretary has been appointed, and it will be his duty to send round a slip every year to each member, asking for changes of address, etc. He will then compile a list of corrections to the Nominal Roll (changes of addresses, deaths, etc.) and send a copy of this and a Christmas card to members.

The annual expenses, it is hoped, will not exceed £25, and will be met by voluntary subscription amongst members. A donation is in no sense obligatory, but any old comrade who cares to subscribe any sum, however small, should send it to the Honorary Secretary.

Another equally important object, for which this Old Comrades Association has been formed, is to provide the means of getting members into touch with other Royal Artillery Associations and Societies, and of bringing to light cases of members or their dependents who may require assistance. Such cases will be reported by the Honorary

Introduction

Secretary to the " Gunners' Friend," 33, Tothill Street, Westminster. The " Gunners' Friend " is connected with the R.A. War Commemoration Fund and other R.A. Societies, and is therefore backed by all the resources of the Regiment.

Any old member of the Battery who is in difficulty, or who needs advice or assistance of any kind, should therefore write to the Secretary, or to any other member of the Battery, officer or otherwise, and tell him of his troubles.

It will be the duty and privilege of every member who knows, or hears of, an old comrade in distress, to give him a helping hand by writing to the Honorary Secretary and acquainting him with the facts.

As far as I myself am concerned, nothing will give me greater pleasure than to hear from any one of my old gunners at any time, more particularly if I can be of any assistance to him.

D. A. SANDFORD.

July, 1919.

CHAPTER I

FORMATION

DECEMBER, 1915—MAY, 1916

THE NUCLEUS. 94 Siege Battery began its existence on December 16th, 1915, when Capt. D. A. Sandford,* who was shortly afterwards promoted Major, arrived at Tynemouth with orders to form a unit of this kind for service overseas. Forty per cent. of the personnel was to consist of Regulars and New Army men belonging to the Tynemouth R.G.A. garrison, while the remainder was furnished by Territorials from the Durham R.G.A. (West Hartlepool). The detachment from the latter unit provided three officers, Capt. A. C. Bennett, Lieut. G. Clark and 2nd Lieut. M. Platnauer. The remaining officers to complete the establishment were 2nd Lieuts. D. M. Cassidy and M. S. Lush, who were posted from Lydd.

TRAINING. Training proceeded apace when once the personnel had arrived, and included infantry drill, physical training, gun drill, battery drill, the construction of dug-outs, and lectures on gunnery, as well as classes for specialists such as signallers (on whose training particular care was bestowed by the O.C.), B.C.A.'s, observers, layers, etc. The officers pursued their studies in the duties of section commanders, map reading, reconnaissance work, the collection and reporting of information, and the working out of targets and

---

* Awarded D.S.O., January, 1916.

15

lines of fire. That the reconnaissance work not infrequently resulted in the observers being mistaken for spies, and reported as such by the local worthies, rather added to than detracted from the common zest.

BEXHILL. On February 4th, 1916, the Battery left for Bexhill (Cooden Camp). The garrison band played the men to the station, where the fair sex mingled and lingered to the last amid a scene of great war enthusiasm. At Cooden, four strenuous weeks were spent and much useful work carried out, including the laying of platforms and the man-handling of guns at night across country and over ditches.

LYDD. On March 8th, the unit was sent to Lydd for seven weeks to complete its training as a Siege Battery. Here practice shooting was carried out under field conditions with 6-inch howitzers. Here, too, for the first time acquaintance was made with the 9·2-inch howitzer, the equipment with which the Battery was subsequently to be armed. The joys and difficulties of mounting and dismounting that armament by night were duly experienced in practice.

ARMING. Towards the end of April, 94, its home-training completed, was sent to Stockcross near Newbury (Berks), where it took over its own guns (four 9·2-inch howitzers, Mark I.) and stores complete, and first beheld its own R.A.S.C. Ammunition Column, consisting of an amazing array of thirty-two 3-ton lorries, four caterpillar tractors,* and one Daimler

---

* The speed of these tractors when drawing a gun, which travelled in three linked-up loads, consisting respectively of the barrel on its transporting wagon, carriage, and bed-plate—a total weight of approximately fifteen tons—averaged about three miles per hour. They were not confined to roads and could travel readily across country. In practice this slow speed was no hindrance, as there was of necessity a great deal of work to be done in preparing positions before they were ready for mounting the guns. The gunners were sent ahead in lorries with the stores, while the guns would arrive later at a pre-arranged hour.

Original Personnel of 94 Siege Battery R.G.A. on proceeding overseas, May, 1916.

light car under 2nd Lieut. R. T. Dunn, R.A.S.C. (M.T.).

FRANCE. Shortly afterwards the guns, stores, caterpillars and lorries, having been sent by road to Avonmouth, were shipped and taken across to Boulogne by 2nd Lieut. Lush and a small party of men. They were there joined by the remainder of the personnel who had crossed from Folkestone on May 30th.

There was naturally considerable excitement among the men at thus finding themselves at length in France, the theatre of war, and at the prospect of shortly going into action. Speculation was rife as to where the first battle-field was likely to be.

CHAPTER II

THE BATTLES OF THE SOMME

JUNE, 1916—MARCH, 1917

THE COMING OFFENSIVE. It shortly transpired that a joint Franco-British offensive on a large scale on both banks of the Somme was in preparation. As far as the British forces were concerned, the main front of attack extended from Maricourt, on the right bank of the Somme, where junction was effected with the French, on the south, as far as the Ancre, in front of St. Pierre Divion, on the north. Subsidiary attacks were to be launched north of the Ancre as far as Gommecourt. The Fourth Army, under Gen. Sir Henry S. Rawlinson, K.C.B., K.C.V.O., held the line between the Somme and Serre, while

B

Gen. Sir E. H. H. Allenby, K.C.B., commanding the Third Army, was responsible for the
remainder. The strategic objects in view, to
quote Field-Marshal Sir Douglas Haig's subsequent
dispatch, were (1) to relieve the pressure on
Verdun ; (2) to assist our Allies, the Italians and
Russians, by preventing a further transfer of
German troops from the Western front ; and
(3) to wear down the strength of the German
forces in France.

THE FIRST POSITION. For this offensive every available
gun was required. 94 accord-
ingly received orders to move, and
proceeded by road to Doullens, while the guns
were sent by rail. Thence a further journey was
made to the village of Bayencourt, where the
Battery was posted to the 35th Heavy Artillery
Group (Lieut.-Col. H. G. Brett), VII. Corps Heavy
Artillery (then commanded by Brig.-Gen. Buckle),
and ordered into action.

A position was at once selected in an orchard
on a by-road leading west from Bayencourt
Church. Here the guns were immediately mounted,
in spite of the unkindness of the elements, on the
night of June 9th—10th. 94 thus found itself
on the extreme left wing of the impending attack.

PREPARATIONS FOR THE BATTLE. The next three weeks were spent
in completing the gun positions,
storing ammunition, constructing
O.P.'s,* and laying to them a net-
work of telephone lines. During training great
emphasis had always been laid by Maj. Sandford
on the extreme importance of efficient communications. This principle, thus early laid down, was
always rigidly adhered to and carried out in the
field. The policy throughout the campaign was that
the Battery must depend, as far as possible, on its

---

* An accepted abbreviation for Observation Posts.

own eyes for the control of fire, as well as on the collection of first-hand information by direct observation of the enemy, and that lines must be maintained, and repaired at all times, and under all circumstances, in order that the information acquired could be transmitted to Battery and Brigade Headquarters without delay.

On paper this seemed easy enough. Under battle conditions the reverse was the case. But this may now be said. The execution of the policy evolved as brave and gallant a band of signallers as any commanding officer could desire. The subsequent narrative provides numerous instances of their individual heroism.

By the third week in June all was ready. Five hundred rounds per gun had been accumulated, which in those days was unheard-of extravagance in 9·2-inch ammunition. A few rounds only were fired for registration purposes in order that the Germans might not suspect the presence of so many new guns. As for the gunners themselves, they were straining at the leash, anxious for the battle to commence. The position was personally inspected by the G.O.C. R.A. VII. Corps, Brig.-Gen. C. M. Ross-Johnson, D.S.O., who expressed his satisfaction with the arrangements, and especially with the system of telephone lines.

PRELIMINARY BOMBARDMENT. On June 24th a seven days' preliminary bombardment began. 94's chief target consisted of a system of trenches from Gommecourt Wood to Rossignol Wood, which were dosed with 200 rounds per day. The Germans responded with energy, and telephone lines were constantly cut. It was during this time that Bdrs. A. Cunningham and A. V. Toop, and Grs. J. H. Collick and G. H. Edser, did some very gallant work mending lines under great danger, thus setting a fine example to their section of individual bravery.

July 1st.—The infantry assault on the Gommecourt salient by the 46th and 56th Divisions
was timed for 7.30 a.m.   This was preceded by an
intense bombardment, which acted as a powerful
safety-valve for war fever among the gunners, who
succeeded in firing 100 rounds per gun in sixty-five
minutes—a most exceptional rate for a 9·2-inch.
Such rapid rates were in fact subsequently dis-
countenanced by the authorities on their finding
that the mechanism became overheated and
buffers and recuperators suffered.

Our infantry succeeded in entering the enemy
trenches at certain points, but met with vigorous
opposition.   Heavy and confused fighting, which
was observed and reported by the F.O.O.'s*
(the Major and 2nd Lieuts. Cassidy and Lush),
continued all day in the first and second German
lines.

The O.P. party were able to turn the guns on to
various bodies of the enemy who were seen massing
for a counter-attack.   The enemy shelling was
very heavy, and telephone lines were continually
being cut.   But owing to the gallantry of Cpl.
D. Jenkins, Bdrs. Cunningham and Toop, and
Grs. J. S. Edwards, J. W. Barr and R. C. Moyes,
such breaks were always quickly repaired in the
face of heavy fire.

The assault here, as already mentioned, was a
subsidiary one, and only intended as a distraction.
As soon as it was considered that it had achieved
this object, our troops, or rather the survivors,
were withdrawn, and further infantry fighting at
this point ceased.   Farther south considerable
success had attended our arms, and the attack was
to be vigorously pressed in that quarter.

On July 2nd an amazing spectacle was seen on
the Gommecourt battle-ground.   A two hours'

* An accepted abbreviation for Forward Observation Officers.

truce had been arranged to enable both sides to collect their wounded and bury their dead. British and Germans were accordingly seen walking about unconcernedly in No Man's Land which but the day before had been an inferno of fire.

A LULL. For the rest of the month (July) the Battery was silent. The time was spent in overhauling the guns, all of whose buffers and recuperators had suffered from the recent rapid rates of fire, and in the preparation of a new position near the village of Hebuterne, about 900 yards behind our front line.

An assault on the Serre Ridge had been planned, and several batteries were to be sited well forward on the northern flank of this attack for counter-battery work. The personnel of 94 worked on the position for three weeks. During this time it constructed several dug-outs, and laid its gun platforms, in spite of the unwelcome attentions of a German machine gunner who was playfully called "Parapet Percy."

CHANGING GUNS. The position, however, was never occupied by the Battery. On August 14th orders were received to hand over the guns and stores *in situ*, as well as the recently prepared position near Hebuterne, to 143 Siege Battery R.G.A., which had just arrived from England. In exchange, the latter's guns and stores, then at Doullens, were to be taken over forthwith. 94 accordingly proceeded to Doullens, and the exchange was effected by August 23rd.

Word then came through to move south to Albert by road. It became evident that the Battery was this time to be used on the main front of attack between the Somme and the Ancre, where the fighting since July 1st had been incessant. All the men were delighted at the prospect of another battle.

Alterations in the personnel had meanwhile

been slight. 2nd Lieut. C. G. Lovegrove had been
posted to the Battery about June 29th. On
August 19th Capt. Bennett received orders to
proceed to England, where new units were being
rapidly formed, and where he was given the command of 186 Siege Battery. Gr. H. Flewker
had, unfortunately, been killed in a railway
accident on July 11th.

FOURTH
ARMY.
On arriving at Albert 94 passed
into Gen. Rawlinson's Fourth
Army, and came under the control
of 45th Heavy Artillery Group (Lieut.-Col. E.
McM. Seddon*), Anzac Corps.

The orders were to go into action at once.
Two days were spent in preparing a position on
the western edge of Contalmaison, a village which
had been captured a few days previously. This
site was subsequently found unsuitable. After
further reconnaissances the two guns of the Right
Section were mounted on August 25th behind the
ruins of La Boisselle Church.

On September 3rd the Left Section moved into
an exposed and advanced position in "Spring
Gardens," a sunken road connecting Ovillers with
the main Albert-Pozières road, and about 1,500
yards west of Pozières. It was here 2,300 yards
behind the front line, and was accordingly allotted
to counter-battery work.

While these positions were being prepared,
Bdr. F. J. McMullen and Grs. J. W. Barr, T.
Eltringham, and A. H. Thomson were killed by
shell-fire.

ANOTHER
BATTLE.
The British attack, in support of
which these guns had been sited,
was fixed for September 15th. The
objective was the rearmost of the enemy's original
systems of defence between Morval and Le Sars,

---

* Subsequently awarded D.S.O.

as well as the village of Courcelette. The preceding days were spent in registration work, and
on September 12th a methodical bombardment was opened and continued uninterruptedly
till 6.20 a.m. on the 15th, when the fire became
intense in support of the assaulting infantry.

PRELIMINARY ATTACK. On September 10th a successful
minor operation took place, which
resulted in the capture of a section
of the German trenches a few hundred yards south
of Pozières Windmill.   The last piece of the crest
of the ridge held by the Germans was wrested
from them, and a very valuable observation of
the ground round Courcelette obtained. 94
carried out a heavy bombardment of this trench
on September 9th and 10th, using visual observation from our own trenches 100 yards away.
The fine work of the signallers on this occasion
was shown by the fact that 94 was the only
battery which had had a line through long enough
before the assault to carry out a bombardment,
or to obtain a registration.   During the intense
artillery fire preceding the attack, another 9·2-inch
battery and one 8-inch battery were ordered to
take part without registration, with the result
that our observation party (under the Major
and Lieut. Lush) was "bracketted" by the
9·2-inch battery, and only the fact that one line
was "through" to the Group, saved our own
trench from being roughly handled.

The most trying part of those preparatory days
was the laying of telephone lines to the O.P.'s on
Pozières Ridge.   The signallers had a most unenviable time, both by day and night, in establishing and maintaining communications.   Lines
were continually cut by shell-fire, and just as
constantly mended at great personal risk.   Thanks
to the gallant work of Cpls. D. Jenkins and R. W.
Crouch, Bdrs. A. Cunningham, W. S. Brice. E.

Carter, and several others, who showed that they
never knew what danger was, the O.P.'s were
always in touch with the Battery, and the Battery
with the Group.

2nd Lieut. Lovegrove distinguished himself in
his endeavours to erect an O.P in Pozières
Windmill, once a very prominent feature, but
reduced to ruins by German guns, who found it
an excellent Datum Point. On his return to the
Battery he and his party ran into a barrage of
gas shells. He had the misfortune to break the
eye-piece of his gas mask, with the result that he
was badly gassed and had to be sent to hospital
the same evening.

The sub-sections, too, had their first experience
of gas shelling, under which they behaved admirably. The Left Section, on one occasion, continued unloading ammunition in their gas masks.
This was largely due to the fine example set by
2nd Lieut. Cassidy, Sgt. A. Nethercott, and Cpls.
A. E. Wright and A. H. Birks. On the afternoon
of September 14th, Lieut. G. Clark, during several
trying hours at the O.P., was wounded and sent
to England.

The outstanding feature of the
THE TANKS. great attack on the following day
was the introduction of our new
engine of war, a heavily armoured caterpillar
car, known as a "Tank." These came as a great
surprise to the enemy, as well as to most of our
own troops, and materially helped the infantry,
whose advance met with immediate success on
almost the whole of the front attacked.

The gun detachments had a strenuous time in
serving the guns, and the O.P. party soon reported
the successful advance of our unassailable tanks,
and the capture of Courcelette and Martinpuich.
Owing to the personal bravery of Cpl. A. V.
Toop, Bdrs. A. Cunningham and E. Carter, and

Grs. J. H. Collick and R. Peppert, who laboured on the lines among continuously bursting shells, communication remained unbroken throughout.

On September 16th 2nd Lieut. Cassidy, while engaged on a reconnaissance, was hit in the shoulder by a piece of 5·9-inch. He refused, however, to remain at the dressing station, and returned to duty a few days later. For their work as F.O.O.'s during these operations, 2nd Lieuts. Cassidy and Lush were awarded the Military Cross.

Reinforcements to replace the officer casualties were however soon forthcoming, and 2nd Lieut. B. H. de Beer joined from England on September 20th, followed two days later by 2nd Lieut. R. A. E. Somerville, M.M. The former was a young New Zealand Field-Gunner. The latter had been promoted on the field to commissioned rank after serving as a Sergeant for a year previously in 30 Siege Battery.

THIEPVAL. On September 26th a successful attack was launched against Thiepval and the defences to the north and east of that village, tanks again co-operating. The enemy resisted stoutly, and the mere mention of such strong points as Mouquet Farm, Stuff and Schwaben Redoubts—will recall the very bitter and desperate fighting that took place.

The Battery's contribution to this operation consisted of the bombardment of Hessian, Regina, and Kenora trench systems, and the villages of Pys, Irles and Miraumont in support of the II. and Canadian Corps.

The Left Section by reason of its advanced position did counter-battery work under Capt. Platnauer with no little success.

The F.O.O. party, under Lieut. Lush, on this occasion experienced a memorable two hours in the front trenches of one of the attacking battalions. A 5·9-inch shell dropped in the trench in which they were observing, killing two infantry-men and burying the three members of the party. Cpl. D. Jenkins and Gr. J. S. Edwards were with some difficulty extricated and handed over to the care of an advanced dressing station, suffering from shell shock. Both these telephonists had done gallant work that day flag-signalling, in spite of snipers and machine-gun fire, back to the main F.O.O. party which was on the Toms Cut Ridge about 1,000 yards in rear.

PRESENTATION OF MEDALS. An interesting ceremony took place in the Right Section position on September 29th, Brig.-Gen. D. F. H. Logan, C.B., C.M.G., then commanding II. Corps H.A., presenting Bdr A. V. Toop with his M.M. ribbon. Toop was warmly complimented by the General on his exceptionally fine performances as telephonist and linesman during the September operations. Bdr. A. Cunningham and Gr. J. H. Collick, who had also been awarded Military Medals, and thus shared with Toop the honour of being the first men of the Battery to gain decorations, had been sent to hospital wounded, and were therefore absent from the parade. Collick subsequently died of pneumonia following a slow recovery from a bad abdominal wound.

He was a fine example of total disregard for personal safety in the performance of duty. He and Bdr. Cunningham were always inseparable and to the fore when there was any heavily shelled piece of line to repair or dangerous O.P. to man. The manner of his being wounded showed the stuff of which he was made. The O.P.—a farm on the main Albert-Bapaume road near Courcelette—was being shelled with 5·9's. The line leading into the O.P. was quickly cut. Without any hesitation Bdr. Toop and Gr. Collick at once left and proceeded to repair the line while the shelling continued. In doing so Collick was badly hit in the stomach. His courage and cheerfulness when being led back—there being no stretchers available—to the dressing station in Courcelette, will ever be remembered by his comrades. He recovered slowly from his wound, but his whole system had been shaken and sapped, and he succumbed to pneumonia in November, 1916.

MINOR OPERATIONS. During October, except for one or two minor attacks in which Regina Trench was captured, active operations on a large scale on this front were suspended, and the Battery entered upon its first winter of active service. But the High Command had decided to continue to harass the enemy, increase his casualties, and deprive him of all ground of any tactical value for us. This process continued intermittently throughout the winter.

About this time a forward position was prepared by parties from both sections under 2nd Lieut. de Beer, 500 yards due north of Courcelette—probably the largest mud-pie the Battery ever made. Though never occupied, it taught all concerned what preparation of a position in winter meant, and none were sorry when it was abandoned.

The difficulties of communication in the minor operations already referred to had also been trebled by the very bad weather which had turned the battle-field into a bog ; and the results obtained by Bdrs. A. V. Toop, E. Carter, and A. H. Birks, Grs. H. Bean, O. Ware and R. Peppert as linesmen were most laudable. No less worthy of mention was the work of the gun detachments under Sgts. L. L. Clarke, R. Winter, A. Nethercott and J. H. Gilmour.

The Battery sustained few losses in this period. Unfortunately they included B.S.M. M. F. Cook, who was injured through falling down into a dug-out. He was subsequently invalided to England, being replaced by B.S.M. G. Marshall.

In connection with the question of casualties it may here be explained that the locating and subsequent neutralisation of hostile batteries had not yet been fully developed by the Germans, who up to this time protected their infantry, for the most part, by barraging their own trenches and bombarding ours. The policy of vigorous counter-battery work, as being in the long run the best protection for infantry, while at the same time the cause of so many casualties to our R.A. personnel, was only fully developed by them in 1917.

Between November 13th-16th Battery Headquarters and the Right Section moved up to join the Left Section at Spring Gardens (Ovillers). Here 2nd Lieut. Lovegrove rejoined from England, having recovered from his gassing on the night of September 11th-12th. The personnel was very comfortably housed in the position in deep dug-outs of their own construction. The detachment quarters and officers' mess were quite a side-show of the district. A part of the Battery had been organised into day and night shifts in order to ensure continuous work on these mining operations.

CHRISTMAS, 1916. A pleasant break in the monotony of this winter campaign came with Christmas Day. By using his exceptional powers of persuasion the O.C. had obtained two Nissen huts. These arrived on December 24th, and by noon on the following day had been erected. The speed with which they were rigged up would have surprised Nissen himself, if such was their inventor's name. Meanwhile the Battery light car (a Daimler) and a lorry had made several excursions into Amiens in search of eatables, and thanks to the efforts of 2nd Lieut. Lovegrove, the men were able to sit down to a very enjoyable meal on Christmas Day.

On February 5th the Battery lost the valuable services of B.Q.M.S. F. W. Murray, one of the most cheery and hardworking of men. The formation of new batteries at home necessitated the withdrawal of experienced N.C.O.'s from France, so that the Q.M.S. and Cpl. A. E. Wright were sent home on promotion. Murray's place was taken by B.Q.M.S. F. C. Finch (Kent R.G.A. (T.)).

ANCRE VALLEY ABANDONED. Between February 4th and 9th, 1917, the Battery moved up to Thiepval, an advance of about 1,000 yards, occupying a position immediately to the east of that village. The move was memorable on account of the hard frost which had prevailed for five previous weeks, and which provided the gunners with an opportunity of doing a little amateur blasting with ammonal in preparing gun pits. No. 4 did a very smart shift, but No. 2 will remember the two days it took them to empty an earth-box, owing to its frozen condition. No. 1 Sub-Section had even worse luck. After six weeks' hard frost a rapid thaw set in on the very night on which they remounted their gun.

While in this position the Battery supported the attacks by the II. Corps against Grandcourt and Miraumont, which, in conjunction with the capture of Beaucourt and the trench systems between that village and Puisieux, drove the enemy out of the Ancre valley and forced them to drop back on Irles and the Loupart line, leaving Grandcourt, Pys and Miraumont in our hands. Gr. W. Holmes was unfortunately killed in these operations.

The enemy retreat, which had
GRANDCOURT. thus assumed marked proportions,
presented peculiar difficulties to the
heavy artillery in their efforts to support our
advancing troops. The roads were impassable
owing to the intense bombardment to which they
had been subjected during the previous seven
months.

But the O.C. determined that the Battery
should not be left behind, and asked and obtained
permission from Gen. Logan to advance across
country. On February 27th he accordingly commenced to move the Right Section from Thiepval
into Grandcourt, over the crater field between
these two points. The operation cannot be
described better than in the words of his report :—

"Between February 25th and March 3rd a
9·2-inch howitzer was hauled by caterpillars from
Thiepval to Grandcourt across two miles of open
country in the neighbourhood of Stuff and Schwaben redoubts, one of the most battered bits of
ground on this portion of the front. The whole
area was covered with shell holes full of water,
and the ground was sodden and treacherous
through the recent thaw.

The sunken Stump Road and numerous
trenches, including Zollern, Hessian and Regina,
were crossed. The tractors, five in all, and their
loads, were constantly bogged, and the work
throughout very arduous and trying to the drivers,
whilst their machines frequently broke down and
had to be repaired in the field."

It was mainly due to the personal efforts of
Sgt. W. H. Denton, R.A.S.C. (i/c caterpillars),
and Sgt. J. Collyer (No. 2 Sub.) that two guns
reached their ultimate positions in Grandcourt.

The ammunition for this site was supplied by a
light railway built by the Left Section with the
assistance of parties from other batteries.

CAPTURE OF LOUPART LINE. Whilst here, these two guns, under 2nd Lieut. Lush, assisted in the operations in which Irles and the Loupart Line were captured. A very successful shoot with aeroplane observation on an active hostile battery near Achiet-le-Grand was accomplished, as proved by subsequent inspection of the position.

The Left Section had meanwhile dismounted and prepared gun pits in Miraumont under 2nd Lieut. de Beer. Owing to the rapidity of the enemy's further retreat, however, these were not occupied.

SOMME BATTLES REVIEWED. Thus ended the first battles of the Somme. In eight months the Fourth and Fifth British Armies under Gens. Sir H. S. Rawlinson and Sir H. de la P. Gough, had blasted their way from Albert to the outskirts of Bapaume, thus further freeing the important nerve-centre of Amiens from the threat of capture. Verdun had been relieved, and the German forces held on the Western Front.

Our artillery power had by now been developed, and had for the first time in the war made itself felt in full force. Not excepting the tentative attacks on small fronts and for short periods at Neuve Chapelle and Loos in 1915, the offensive on the Somme was by far the most ambitious blow that the British had struck since the war began.

Progress had been slow but sure. Every obstacle standing in the way of our infantry was first destroyed by shell storms. Whole villages were thus obliterated. Trenches were flattened. Wire entanglements were swept away. Not a tree escaped the avalanche. The whole country-side had been drenched with shell-fire, and the ground scarred and seared with a bewildering

maze of trenches and shell craters. The enemy
had been forced into a salient on the north flank
of the battle-field from which they soon found
themselves obliged to withdraw.

This section of the history cannot be closed
without a word of admiration for the courage and
endurance displayed by all ranks, ''subjected
as they were,'' in the words of Sir Douglas Haig,
''to the maximum of personal hardship · and
physical strain through a long summer and winter
campaign of unusual severity.''

CHAPTER III

Subsequent German Retreat to the Hindenburg Line and Battle of Arras

March—May, 1917

RETREAT TO HINDENBURG LINE. For some time prior to the conclusion of these Somme battles, indications that the area of the German withdrawal would be extended to both flanks had been accumulating. Indeed, the retreat turned out to be part of a carefully organised plan, which had been forced upon them by our Somme successes, to retire to a new system of defences known to the British as the ''Hindenburg Line,'' and by March 12th, 1917, that retirement was in full swing.

In the north this retreat hinged on the village of Tilloy-lez-Mofflaines, about one kilometre south-east of Arras. It included the abandonment on the British front of Bapaume, Peronne and Roisel.

The previous devastation of the country and the destruction of everything that could be of any

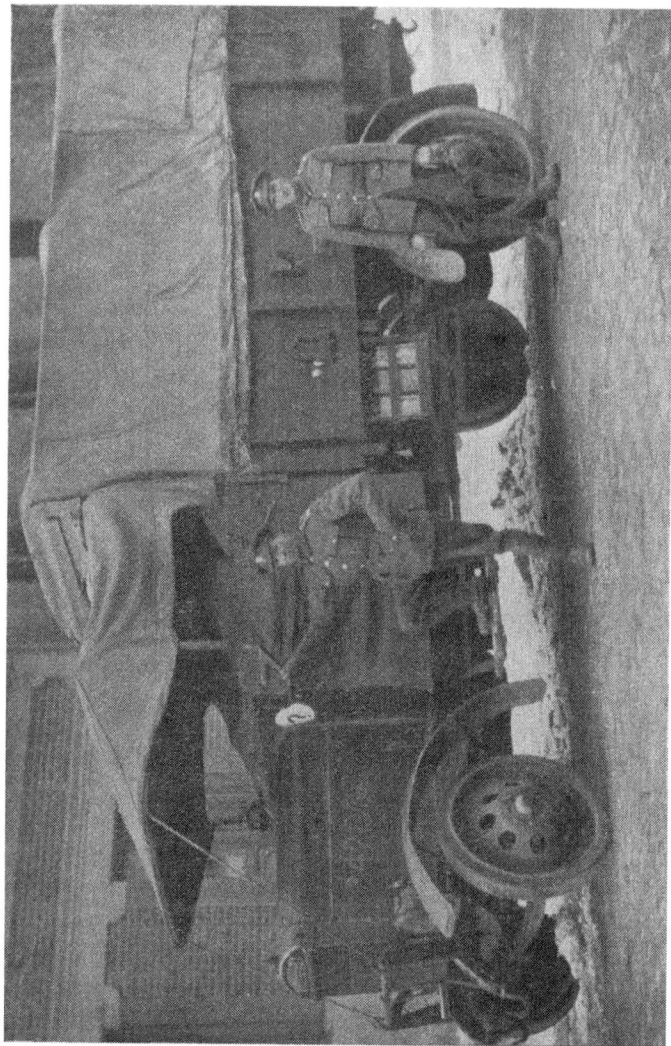

THORNYCROFT "J" TYPE 3½-TON LORRY (30–35 H.P.).
Maximum load of 9·2-inch ammunition, 20 complete rounds.

use to his pursuers, the blowing up of bridges and roads, the setting of innumerable time-fuse, clockwork, acid, and mechanical exploding devices and ''booby traps '' to hinder pursuit, and inflict casualties on our advancing troops, were prominent features of the enemy retreat. The new German line, which had been carefully prepared, ran approximately east of Arras, Queant, and St. Quentin.

The foregoing conditions, coupled with the wet weather, rendered a further advance of the Siege Artillery exceedingly difficult, even when possible. The only practicable road for heavy traffic was the main Albert-Bapaume-Cambrai road. Accordingly some only of the heavy guns were pushed forward in pursuit.

OUT OF ACTION.
94 was ordered to ''stand easy,'' and found itself out of action for the next ten days (March 18th–28th).

INDIVIDUAL EXPLOITS.
During this period, however, Maj. Sandford, Capt. F. Grant* and 2nd Lieut. Lush combined the duties of Artillery Liaison Officer with the infantry, and Reconnaissance Officer for the II. Corps H.A., and sent in valuable reports to those Headquarters from the front lines.

The telephonists under Bdr. Toop again rose to the occasion, and at one time had the only heavy artillery line into the forward area. This meant laying and maintaining ten to thirteen miles of cable. Capt. Grant was with our advanced patrols at the capture of Achiet-le-Grand. Seeing that our infantry were being held up at the eastern exit of the village by some Germans in a trench, he secured a Lewis gun. With this he clambered up the ruins of the church and fired on the enemy, driving them off.

---

* For this officer's posting, see following paragraph.

C

Meanwhile there had been several changes in personnel and command. On February 9th, Capt. M. Platnauer was posted to 45th H.A.G. as Adjutant, Capt. F. Grant (North Scottish R.G.A. (T.)), relinquishing that position and joining the Battery. 2nd Lieut. D. M. Cassidy also left on posting to IV. Corps Counter-Battery Staff. During March and April the Battery passed successively from 45th H.A.G. to 10th H.A.G., II. Corps, thence to 40th H.A.G., V. Corps, and when finally in position again (at Vaulx-Vrau-court) was attached to 25th H.A.G. (Lieut.-Col. S. O. Boyd), V. Corps, Fifth Army.

BATTLE OF ARRAS. By April 6th the Battery was once more in action, this time on the north-western outskirts of Vaulx-Vraucourt, four miles N.N.E. of Bapaume.

The advance party of the Left Section under 2nd Lieuts. de Beer and Somerville were shelled when moving in, and lost two lorries that were set on fire and destroyed, though the stores were salved in time.

A steady bombardment of the Hindenburg Line was now begun, and on April 11th the V. Corps, in conjunction with the I. Anzac Corps, attacked the enemy lines near Bullecourt. This attack formed the right flank of the major operations of the First and Third Armies on the left, which resulted in the capture of the Vimy Ridge and the piercing of the Hindenburg Line in front of Arras.

A very fine example of endurance was the twenty-four hours' barrage in which the Battery took part in support of that battle. Opening fire at Zero (5 a.m.) on the 11th, they continued at varying rates until 5 a.m. on the 12th without ceasing fire. About 1,200 rounds were expended, and no single gun was out of action for more than two hours. This was due to the care and attention displayed by the Nos. 1 and the artificers.

By a surprise attack on April 15th, the enemy caused a diversion against the I. Anzac Corps on the right, between Noreuil and Lagnicourt, but the lost ground was recovered by a counter-attack the same morning. The C.O. was asked to obtain some information on the situation on the morning of that day, and the subsequent reconnaissance and report by Capt. Grant was the subject of a congratulatory letter from Brig.-Gen. T. R. C. Hudson, D.S.O., Commanding Heavy Artillery V. Corps.

SPRING CONDITIONS. The stay at Vaulx-Vraucourt brought with it a welcome improvement in the material conditions of the Battery. Winter had now given way to spring, and work amid surroundings not yet blasted by the hand of war was a striking and very pleasant contrast to life among the devastated Somme battle-fields. To be able to kick a football once again, on a level stretch of green turf was another novelty which delighted the gunners.

The remainder of the month, and up to the middle of May, was chiefly occupied by counter-battery work, enlivened by occasional sniping at wagons and enemy movement, as seen by the F.O.O.'s from the Cemetery O.P. near Ecoust. Several further attempts were also made to breach the Hindenburg Line and capture Bullecourt.

Casualties since the New Year had been very low. They were Gr. W. F. Holtham, killed at Grandcourt in April, and Grs. W. H. Smith and G. E. Maddocks at Vaulx-Vraucourt. Some six others were wounded. The New Year's "Gazette," published at this time, included a "mention" for Maj. Sandford. Promotion accounted for Sgt. Nethercott's departure about the end of March, by which the Battery lost another stalwart, though such changes as these gave younger N.C.O.'s the opportunity to justify

their selection.   Cpls. Harrison and Brignall,
Bdrs. Smith, Price, Lodge, Porrett, Trueman and
Bate are but a few of the men whose soldierly
conduct was noticeable, and who were destined to
maintain the reputation of the Battery in the
later stages of its history.

CHAPTER IV

The Battle of Messines

June, 1917

TRANSFER
TO SECOND
ARMY.

On May 19th the Battery pulled
out of position and was withdrawn
to Albert, where it entrained some
days later for Bailleul, on posting
to II. Anzac Corps, Second Army.

By May 25th it was again in action under the
orders of 52nd H.A.G. (Lieut.-Col. E. Wighton,
D.S.O.), in a prepared position at Dou-dou Farm,
about 1,000 yards west of Ploegsteert.

It soon became obvious that a " show " was
in preparation.   The objective of Gen. Sir
H. C. O. Plumer (Commanding Second Army)
proved to be none other than the famous Messines
Ridge, which had remained in German hands since
November, 1914, and formed a prominent natural
feature in the flat country around Ypres.   Our
position in the " Salient " had always been
dominated by it.   With the Menin and Aubers
ridges on its north and south, it formed an integral
part of the German defences in Flanders.   While
affording to the enemy ready ground observation
over our lines, it denied to us any such advantage,
and increased the difficulties of preparation for
our attack.   The outstanding feature of the

assault on this position, which took place on June
7th, was the firing of an extensive series of very
powerful land mines, which had taken many
months to prepare, and whose final explosion
resembled a miniature earthquake.

During the week prior to the battle the enemy
artillery had been extremely active in counter-
battery bombardment, and hardly a night passed
without its quota of gas shelling. The occasion
is thus noteworthy as being the second time the
Battery was subjected to this particular form of
German " strafing." Many of the batteries in
the immediate vicinity had their ammunition
dumps destroyed, but fortunately 94 escaped.
1st A./M. C. J. Sheward, R.A.F., the Battery's
efficient wireless operator, will doubtless remember the six-inch shell which, as the result of a
direct hit on a neighbouring dump, was hurled
through the air several hundred yards and crashed
through his dug-out, but happily failed to explode.

BATTLE   In the artillery preparation for
OF   the attack, the Battery's targets,
MESSINES.   " Ulna Switch " and " Ulrica Support," received such attention that it
was impossible to identify them on going over the
captured ground later on. In the actual battle,
it supported the 1st New Zealand Division, by
participating in the heavy artillery barrage
through Messines.

The assault proved eminently successful, and
the Messines ridge passed into our hands, as a
result of one of the best conceived and most
brilliantly executed attacks so far standing to the
credit of the British Army.

F.O.O.'s.   Work in the Battery had been
very strenuous, but all detachments
acquitted themselves creditably.
Most of the targets were engaged by visual
observation. All the officers participated in this

work, and could take credit for some very successful shooting. Lieut. Lush established an observation post on the Messines ridge shortly after its capture, and by his reports, reliable as usual, kept Headquarters in touch with the progress of operations.

Communication would have been impossible, but for the personal efforts of Bdrs. A. H. Birks and W. S. Edwards. The courage and determination of the telephonists under these N.C.O.'s was also worthy of mention. For his conspicuous gallantry and devotion to duty, Birks was awarded the Belgian " Décoration Militaire," the first foreign honour falling to the Battery.

LE BIZET. A re-siting of our artillery followed shortly after the battle, and the Battery was accordingly moved 1½ miles south-eastwards into Le Bizet, a suburb of Armentières. The very dry weather made it possible for the guns to be placed on the banks of the river Lys, where they were mounted on June 10th.

The stay there was short and quiet, but memorable, inasmuch as the enemy was successfully deceived as to the Battery's exact whereabouts, to judge by his persistent shelling of an old unoccupied position about 200 yards away. On June 18th the Battery was withdrawn for a well-earned rest at Neuf Berquin, west of Estaires. Apart from the " stand easy " at Thiepval in March, owing to the THE FIRST REST. impossibility of following up the enemy, this was the first rest the Battery had enjoyed since its arrival in France, and proved very welcome after twelve months' continuous action.

The only casualties in the Messines area were Gr. O. H. Balls, killed, and two men wounded through a stray shell bursting in the Le Bizet position, while Gr. W. Campbell was killed on the night the Battery moved out to rest.

Throughout the whole of the Messines operation Capt. Grant had been detached for duty at II. Anzac Corps H.A. Headquarters as Liaison Officer with the infantry, and did not return until the withdrawal of the Battery to the rest area.

Whilst at Neuf Berquin the guns went into workshops for a very necessary overhaul. B.S.M. G. Marshall left the Battery and was replaced by B.Q.M.S. W. Gilpin. The personnel passed the time pleasantly in games of football, trips in motor lorries to neighbouring towns to see the local concert parties and cinemas, and sundry other amusements beloved of the gunner fresh from the line. Paris was visited by a few of the luckier officers.

On June 23rd the Battery was inspected by Lieut.-Gen. Sir A. J. Godley, K.C.B., K.C.M.G., then commanding II. Anzac Corps. He complimented Major Sandford on the smartness of the parade, and thanked all ranks for their efforts towards making the battle of Messines the success which it was.

CAMOUFLAGE

One of the most important functions of the artillery during the war was to conceal guns from view of the enemy. In the course of this narrative little mention has been made of the Battery's efforts in this respect, and it may therefore be well at this stage to touch upon a few aspects of the subject.

In every position the Battery occupied some form of camouflage was erected or used. The guns themselves were always painted in bold irregular patches—usually yellow, white, and green, a form of dazzle painting which deceived the eye by distorting the shape, thus aiding the process of assimilation to surroundings. This type of camouflage was only efficacious against direct visual observation.

When aerial photography came into vogue an entirely new set of conditions arose. The airman's eyes might not be able to detect the presence of guns, even when flying over them at 1,500 feet. But the photograph he could take when flying at 4,000 to 6,000 feet might reveal their location.

The fact was that these photographs showed up, on development :

(1) The black shadow cast by the guns or their emplacements ;

(2) The break-up of surroundings due to the alterations in surface caused by the guns ;

(3) The tracks through grass leading up to them ;

(4) The " blast " marks immediately in front of the guns caused by the scorching of grass through firing. These marks assumed a regular circular shape. In a photograph the difference in tone between the scorched and unscorched grass was very noticeable. The reason for this is that scorched grass, being shorter and less thick than the unburnt grass further away, has fewer shadows on its surface, and consequently appears lighter in tone ;

(5) All newly dug up earth caused in mounting the guns in their emplacements, or in the erection of any earthworks in the battery position, such as dug-outs, cartridge recesses, slit trenches,* etc. All such earth shows up *white* in photography, because,

---

* Narrow trenches dug close to the guns in which detachments might take cover when under fire.

Holt Caterpillar Tractor (75 h.p.).
Haulage load, 30 tons.

having no shadow casters, such as grass, on its surface, it reflects light rays readily.

It must be understood that a *picture of a gun* rarely, if ever, came out in an aerial photograph. Its presence was *deduced* from one or other of the effects above set forth, or a combination thereof. In fact, the interpretation of aeroplane photographs became an engrossing study by itself, on which specially trained men were employed.

Thus, the problem for the gunner how best to conceal his guns, became one of counteracting by artificial means these effects of light, shade, and tone in aerial photography, which, from interpretation and inference, might reveal the location of his battery to the enemy.

To this end a Camouflage Officer was appointed to the heavy artillery of each Corps. Usually an artist, he was always ready with advice, and— what was more important for the practical gunner who had to reconcile art-theories with the exigencies of action, and the unwieldy size of a 9·2-inch howitzer—he held the keys of the store of camouflage material available for issue.

This mainly consisted of rolls of

(1) Wire or fish netting on to which small strips of coloured canvas had been knotted in varying degrees of thickness.

(2) Coloured material usually of a canvas texture, called " scrim."*

The latter was used for " blanketing " guns, shells, and other objects, by covering them up with this material without any structural support. For reasons already explained this method could only be efficacious on broken ground, amongst ruins, and under trees, etc., where irregularities of surface were already sufficiently marked to ensure the production of black shadows in a

---

* Coco-nut matting was another form sometimes available.

photograph, and where the addition of a few more would not excite suspicion.

The wire netting, however, had to be erected on poles and generally well supported over the gun and its emplacement. The object was to create a perfectly flat overhead cover (which in plan should symmetrise with the surroundings), and which would conceal the black shadows cast by the gun and all earthworks in or near the pit. That cover, in fact, aimed at the production of another surface which should have the effect of absorbing and reflecting about the same amount of light as the surrounding grass, and consequently appear of the same tone in a photograph. For this purpose the canvas strips had to be gradually thinned, or become transparent, towards the outer edges.

Some positions lend themselves naturally to concealment. Others—bare, exposed, and· isolated—are correspondingly difficult to camouflage. The Battery had experience of both types. It was always found that the most effective concealment lay in assimilation to surroundings, for which purpose the natural material ready to hand was often the best for the assumption of a disguise suggested by the environment. In most cases, however, netting was erected over the guns.

In general, the work in connection with camouflaging absorbed much time and energy. The obliteration or extension of existing tracks running into a battery position, and the avoidance of fresh ones, was a study in itself. In addition to the guns, there were cartridge recesses, " slit " trenches, shells, detachment dug-outs,* signal exchange, section posts, command post, officers' quarters, cookhouses and other erections to conceal—a small township in fact.†

---

* Usually an " elephant " iron.
† These conditions were not so aggravated in moving warfare.

Fortunately, as a rule, there was plenty of material available. Indeed, if the authorities told the public how much money was expended on camouflage during the war, much surprise would probably be caused. But the gunner himself knows how wisely and well it was employed.

CHAPTER V

OPERATIONS ON THE FLANDERS COAST

JUNE—DECEMBER, 1917

TO THE COAST. About this time the British line was extended to the coast, our troops relieving the French and Belgians who had hitherto been responsible for the Nieuport sector. Leaving Neuf Berquin under orders on June 27th, the Battery proceeded by road to Oost Dunkirke on the Belgian coast, resting for a night at St. Marie Cappel (near Cassel) and Wormhoudt respectively. There it joined the XV. Corps in Fourth Army, coming under the command of Brig.-Gen. C. W. Collingwood, C.M.G., D.S.O., commanding XV. Corps H.A.

Preparation of a position was at once commenced under orders from 1st H.A.G. (Lieut.-Col. R. N. Lockhart, D.S.O.), and by July 4th Nos. 1, 2 and 4 guns were in action about 2,000 yards east of Oost Dunkirke, on the north side of the road running from that village to Nieuport Bains. The section officers will remember the peculiar difficulties encountered in mounting, in this exposed position on the sand dunes, to avoid detection by enemy aircraft—the only available working space behind the gun platforms being the width of a sandy track running at right angles to the pits. The position was inspected on July 7th by Brig.-Gen. Collingwood, and on the following day by Brig.-Gen. B. R. Kirwan, C.M.G., commanding XV. Corps R.A., who expressed his satisfaction with the excellent camouflage and general arrangements.

Major Sandford was detached from the Battery on July 9th to act as assistant to the Counter-Battery Staff Officer, XV. Corps, a post he held until October 1st. Capt. Grant accordingly assumed temporary command of 94.

PROJECTED OPERATIONS. The offensive operations which had been contemplated in this sector by our High Command, and for which accordingly the heavy artillery had been strongly reinforced, were to some extent forestalled by a successful enemy attack on July 10th, when we lost the right bank of the Yser, from Nieuport to the sea, thus depriving us of essential " jumping off " places.

It is possible that the course of subsequent operations was materially affected by the loss of this ground. But throughout the six following weeks the British artillery maintained an extremely heavy and destructive fire on the German positions and the concreted gun-emplacements defending the coast and Ostend. These demonstrations were mainly intended to support the major operations about to be carried out on the right flank by the First French Army, and the Fifth and Second British Armies.

LOSS OF 2ND LIEUT. B.H.DE BEER Throughout the day of the German attack (July 10th) the Battery was subjected to a severe neutralisation, but all S.O.S. calls were answered with an expenditure of about 700 rounds. Casualties were regrettably high. 2nd Lieut. de Beer, acting as F.O.O., was killed early in the

morning in the O.P. at Nieuport, a shell striking
the loophole through which he was observing.
Later in the day Capt. Grant went out to
recover the body, which he succeeded in doing.
Grs. H. Kellet and A. V. Day were killed, and
six others wounded while helping Capt. Grant
in his search.

The loss of this gallant officer cast a gloom
over the entire Battery. Always keen and ener-
getic, possessing a thorough knowledge of his
work, with a strong sense of humour, and ever
ready to throw off his tunic and handle the shovel
if necessary, he had alike gained the confidence
of his seniors and endeared himself to his men.
Among his brother officers, to whom he was
affectionately known as " Benjy," he left a gap
that was never completely filled.

The six succeeding weeks, during which the
Battery came under the orders of 36th H.A.G.
(Lieut.-Col. A. P. Liston-Foulis,* R.M.A.), wit-
nessed, as has been pointed out, the most extra-
ordinary artillery duel of the war. Owing to the
heavy casualties they were indeed the darkest
days of the Battery's history, and yet, relieved
as they were by many individual and collective
acts of heroism, must rank among the proudest.

BURNING AMMUNITION. On the night of July 10th–11th the
Battery ammunition dump, situated
in a small orchard about fifty yards
square, and containing 1,000 rounds, was set on
fire by enemy shelling, and in a few minutes the
conflagration extended to some small barns flank-
ing the orchard filled with gun stores.

A party of volunteers—headed by Lieuts. Lush
and Somerville, and consisting of Sgt. C. F.
Duckels, Grs. J. L. Price and T. Armitage of
No. 1 Sub-Section, and Sgt. J. Collyer, Grs. F. R.

* Since killed.

Rose, J. Dodd, and R. W. Moore of No. 2 Sub-
Section, and possibly one or two others whose
names it has been impossible to ascertain—
succeeded, in spite of burning and exploding
ammunition, in salving some cartridges and gun
stores and getting the fire under control. The
blaze had meanwhile attracted a little more
enemy shelling, though this could not stay the
efforts of the amateur firemen who, after putting
out a few subsequent minor outbreaks, retired at
dawn, more like sweeps than soldiers. During this
affair Lieut. Somerville surpassed even his usual
sang-froid by extinguishing the flames of a burning
9·2-inch shell.

For this act he was awarded the M.C., Lieut.
Lush receiving a bar to his M.C., while Sgt.
Collyer also added another to his M.M., and Grs.
Dodd and Armitage received the M.M.

MORE
AWARDS.
Two days later (July 12th), whilst
engaging a hostile battery with
aeroplane observation, the veterans
of the Somme, Bullecourt, and Messines again
gave evidence of their ability to face shell-fire.
Shortly after the shoot commenced, an enemy
4·2-inch howitzer battery retaliated with an extremely accurate neutralising fire at the rate of
about four rounds per minute. Both guns (Nos.
2 and 4) continued firing for $1\frac{1}{2}$ hours, when a
shell wounded four of the detachment and damaged
No. 4's breech, thus putting it out of action. No.
2 continued firing for $1\frac{1}{4}$ hours more until the aeroplane went home, having been hit by anti-aircraft
fire. A second plane was at once sent up, and No. 2
opened fire again. After seventeen rounds it was
put out of action, though not before it had obtained
four directs hits on its target. No. 4's damage
having been repaired, a third plane was sent up
to complete the shoot. The gun was shelled as
soon as it opened fire, yet it managed to hit its

target after about twenty rounds, and the plane
went home. During the day the ammunition of
both guns was set on fire.

In his report Capt. Grant remarked: ''The
shooting of both guns was very good throughout,
and the detachments behaved with the greatest
gallantry and determination.'' Meanwhile the
aeroplane had reported that the battery had
been neutralised while engaging its target, and
the Corps Commander called for a report on the
shoot. The result was that the Nos. 1 concerned,
Sgts. J. Collyer and J. H. Gilmour, and the layers
Grs. H. R. Rusby and F. R. Rose, received the
M.M. for this very fine example of collective
bravery.

Casualties were again high. Cpl. J. Mason
and Gr. A. H. Cox were killed and twelve others
wounded. Reinforcements were soon supplied
and 2nd Lieuts. E. S. Hopkins and L. S. Mason
joined on July 14th, from England, followed a few
days later by the requisite number of other ranks.

A NEW
POSITION.
Owing, however, to the havoc
recently created by enemy fire in
the Battery position, another site
was selected about 600 yards in rear, into which
the guns were accordingly moved between July
13th and 15th.

Statistics are very dry reading, but the Battery
War Diary reveals some interesting facts concerning the tale of these three months (July 10th—
September 10th). In this period the Battery
occupied three positions in the same neighbourhood, fired some fifty destructive shoots on hostile
batteries (each averaging about 150 rounds) and
expended 2,000 rounds on S.O.S. calls and trench
bombardments. Owing, however, to the advantages of visual observation afforded by the
dunes in the enemy country, it suffered not a
little. The equivalent of fourteen guns was put

out of action, necessitating in most cases their with-drawal to the Army Heavy Workshops, and for one week in September the Battery consisted of only one gun. Neutralisation by the enemy was often prompt though not always accurate, and on several occasions he attempted a destructive shoot on the Battery of about 200 rounds.

MORE CASUALTIES. It was, however, the short irre-gular concentration, which caught the personnel unawares in the open, that caused most of the casualties. On August 13th Capt. Grant, in his anxiety to see that all were under cover, was badly wounded above the knee by a shell splinter, with the result that he was sent to England, subsequently losing his leg and being invalided out of the service.

The award of an M.C. to him in the next New Year's Honours list gave great satisfaction to all ranks. During the six months he had been with the Battery his ardent spirit had fired all who came into contact with him. A great thruster, gifted with fine abilities and boundless energy, it was hoped that he would later on get opportunities affording wider scope for his talents. That this was not to be proved a keen disappointment to his friends. On his depar-ture Lieut. Lush was appointed Captain, and, in the absence of Major Sandford, temporarily assumed command.

Similar spells of shelling accounted for the death of many others—mostly Battery originals. Those killed were Wh./Gr. E. Mayes (a most efficient craftsman), Sgt. C. F. Duckels, Ftr./Gr. F. T. Freeman, Grs. R. Ryder and J. S. Edwards, the Battery dispatch-riders, and Grs. J. A. Newby, F. Cason, B. Caddick, H. O. Wayman, W. A. Dorrington, and G. H. Edser. About forty-five others were wounded. It was a striking tribute to the efficient way in which the men had built

B.L. 9·2-INCH HOWITZER (MARK I.) IN LOADING POSITION (REAR VIEW).

This photograph is taken from the official handbook of the gun, and reproduced by the special and courteous permission of the Controller of His Majesty's Stationery Office.

their dug-outs that, in spite of several being struck, none were blown in. No. 3 Sub-Section will remember the 8-inch that made an almost successful attempt on theirs.

Meanwhile life out on the lines had been equally dangerous for the telephonists. Every man did his appointed task well, but the code names of the O.P.'s, *e.g.*, "L.T." in the Dunes, and "M.R." in Nieuport, will remind the F.O.O.'s of the splendid work done by Cpl. A. H. Birks, Bdrs. H. Lee, C. J. Small, J. Pritchard, Grs. T. Dakin, A. Houldsworth, J. Dunn, W. S. Brice, and G. Roberts. For reasons already stated "those command post people" were equally busy, and Cpl. R. C. Lodge, Bdr. W. H. Davies and Gr. W. M. Dakers earned high praise for their work.

A SHORT HOLIDAY. By September the duel had been almost broken off and life become more bearable. On September 24th the personnel were withdrawn, leaving the guns under a guard, to the XV. Corps Rest Camp in the Dunes near Zuydcoote. Accommodated in tents about 200 yards from the sea, they passed the five days very pleasantly. Swimming, football and other games were indulged in, and Dunkirke was within easy walking distance. The general verdict on leaving was "a splendid holiday."

The resumption of work saw several changes. On October 2nd Major Sandford rejoined for duty from the Corps Counter-Battery Staff. He had performed his duties whilst there with his customary energy and ability, and the award to him of a "mention" in the New Year's Honours Gazette of 1918 caused no surprise.

A few days later the Battery was further strengthened by the posting of 2nd Lieut. R. Hoggan from 133 Siege Battery, and 2nd Lieut. J. Gardiner from England. On October 5th, 36th

D

H.A.G. was withdrawn, and the Battery passed
to 45th H.A.G., now commanded by Lieut.-Col.
C. E. Inglis, D.S.O., old friends of the Somme
days.

ANOTHER
POSITION.

A change in position occurred
at the same time and the Battery
moved into a site recently vacated
by 133 Siege Battery on the Nieuport-Oost-
Dunkirke road, a move of about 1,000 yards
southwards. It was subsequently shelled there,
though the enemy's efforts were mostly of a harassing nature. The remaining days in the Nieuport
sector were quite uneventful except for the arrival
of 2nd Lieut. W. R. Clarke from England on
October 23rd, and the attachment of Capt. Lush to
XV. Corps R.A. Staff on October 27th. B.Q.M.S.
F. C. Finch was promoted B.S.M. at this time,
his vacancy being filled by B.Q.M.S. R. Collinson.

On October 25th the Battery received a visit
from the O.C.'s brother, Lieut. R. D. Sandford,
R.N., on leave from the Grand Fleet. This
gallant officer subsequently won the V.C. by
blowing up the Mole at Zeebrugge, a story
of heroism familiar to all. His four days'
"leave" in the Battery was not without incidents. The first of these occurred three minutes
after his arrival, and before introductions were
over. A shell dropped a few yards from him, and
was followed by another which blew in the dug-
out intended for his accommodation.

A most unfortunate casualty occurred on
November 24th. During a slight spell of harassing fire Sgt. Collyer and Gr. H. W. Jenson were
killed by a shell striking a cottage in which they
were housed. The loss of Sgt. Collyer was a hard
blow, for by his death the Battery lost a good old
regular of the best type—the ideal No. 1 and
"father" of his detachment.

By the end of November a readjustment of

our Armies had taken place, and the coastal sector was handed back to the French (minus the potatoes), a battery of 150-mm. guns taking over 94's position.   Proceeding by road, the Battery arrived at Wormhoudt on December 6th for a rest and badly needed re-fit.

AN INSPECTION.   Before leaving the XV. Corps the Battery was inspected on parade by Brig.-Gen. Collingwood and highly complimented on the work it had done.

What recollections will come back to all by the mention of those days in the Dunes !   Some memories will be sad through the inevitable results of war, others—more happy—of recreation and amusement, and yet others of work and duty well done in spite of fierce opposition.   But the proudest must surely be the little corner of Coxyde Cemetery, " which is for ever England." The whole experience only tended to deepen the sense of comradeship between officers and men, and the mutual esteem and confidence on which true discipline is based.

The Battery's total casualties while in this sector were about 110 of all ranks.

CHAPTER VI

YPRES AND THE WINTER OF 1917–18

DECEMBER, 1917—MARCH, 1918

CHRISTMAS, 1917.   Arriving at Wormhoudt on December 6th the Battery moved into billets there.   Giving the personnel a few days' rest, the O.C. immediately turned to the very necessary question of training

the large batch of reinforcements (nearly 100 in
all) that had been posted in the previous three
months, and except for a little break at Christmas
it was a busy time for all. '' When are we going
back into the line for a rest ?'' was an invariable
question from some of the Battery wags, and
notwithstanding comfortable billets and the
various attractions of life in a town behind the
lines, the majority seemed quite eager to go into
action again at the beginning of January.

BRIGADES R.G.A. Meanwhile a reorganisation of the
heavy artillery had been in pro-
gress by substitution of the Brigade
for the Group system as heretofore. The obvious
advantages of being permanently under the same
Brigade Commander, and of being continuously
associated with the same sister batteries, did
much to promote an increased *esprit de corps*. On
joining the XIX. Corps (Fourth Army) the Battery
was accordingly posted to the 23rd Heavy Artillery
Brigade R.G.A., commanded by Lieut.-Col. W. N.
Budgen, D.S.O., under whom it remained until the
conclusion of hostilities. The other batteries of
the Brigade were 41, 327 and 355 Siege Batteries
—all 6-inch howitzers.

THE SALIENT. By January 6th the Battery was
once more in action in a position
about 100 yards east of the Yser
Canal Locks at Hetsas. The preparation of this
position entailed a great deal of very arduous
work. It was situated in the vicinity of the old
German front line that had been battered by three
successive years of shelling, while the laying of
platforms and the construction of a very necessary road into the position, under weather conditions quite normal for winter in Flanders, were
some of the difficulties that had to be surmounted.
In particular, the roadway duly constructed was
a monument to the energy of Lieut. Lovegrove,

Sgts. F. Harrison and E. Carter, and their Sub-
Sections Nos. 1 and 2.

CONVERSION
TO 6-GUN
BATTERY.
Very little firing was done in this
position, as the operations round
Passchendaele were now suspended.
The outstanding feature was the
addition of a third section to the Battery, thus
making it a 6-gun unit. 2nd Lieut. G. C. L.
Chamberlain and fifty-four other ranks, together
with guns, stores and mechanical transport, were
taken over on January 15th, 1918, on posting from
190 Siege Battery, which latter, among others,
had been split up to effect this regrouping of 9·2-
inch batteries. The new section was not placed
in position, as orders were received on January
25th to stand by to move. Nos. 3 and 4 guns now
became Centre Section, and the guns of the new
Left Section were numbered 5 and 6.

BACK TO
THE SOMME.
On February 9th, after one month
in the Salient, the Battery and the
remainder of the Brigade entrained
at Poperinghe on being posted to the Fifth Army
(Gen. Sir H. de la P. Gough, K.C.B., K.C.V.O.),
and arrived at Roisel on February 10th. Here
it was attached to Cavalry Corps H.A. for a short
time, and subsequently passed to XIX. Corps
H.A.

Positions were at once prepared on the
southern outskirts of Roisel, the Left and Right
Sections being on the Roisel-Bernes road, and the
Centre Section on the Roisel-Hancourt road.
The personnel was accommodated in cellars in the
village. The only noteworthy features of these
positions were the extremely deep gun pits of the
Left and Right Sections, who had to excavate
into a solid bank, and vied with each other in their
ingenious attempts at revetment, while the unusual
camouflage of the Centre Section, who had erected
structures that at a distance, might be mistaken

for hutments. They were promptly nicknamed
the " Y.M.C.A."

NEW POSITIONS.   From these positions, selected for
defensive reasons, the guns could
not reach beyond the main German
line, and they had hardly been completed when
fresh orders—reflecting a change in the policy of
the Higher Command, owing to the undoubted
indications of an impending German attack on a
large scale—necessitated the siting of the guns
further forward.

About February 29th, therefore, the Left
Section, under Lieut. Somerville, moved into the
valley of the Cologne River about mid-way between
Roisel and Templeux-le-Guerard. A few days
later the Right Section were sent into the Bois
Haut about 500 yards north of Hesbecourt, which
was then merely a small clump of undergrowth.
The shifting of the Centre Section under Lieut.
Lovegrove, ever a glutton for work, into a small
quarry about 400 yards south-east of Hesbecourt,
was a brilliant piece of work. They commenced
to dismount at about 4 p.m. on March 13th, and
by 11 a.m. next morning had not only completed
mounting, but had fired 100 rounds on a bridge
across the St. Quentin Canal.

Major Sandford had meanwhile established his
Headquarters and Command Post on a hill overlook-
ing the Left and Right Sections about 300 yards
west of the latter. But as all sections were so
widely distributed, the distance apart averaging
1,000 yards, the difficulties of efficient central
control were increased, and greater responsibility
than usual was thrown on the Section Commanders. This point is emphasised in view of
the dramatic events of the following week.*

---

* On March 19th, B.Q.M.S. R. Collinson was posted away on
promotion, and Sgt. J. Gilmour became B.Q.M.S. in his place.

CHAPTER VII

MARCH 21ST, 1918, AND SUBSEQUENT BRITISH RETREAT

MARCH—APRIL, 1918

A DEFENSIVE POLICY.   The British High Command had long been aware of the transfer of German troops from Russia to the Western front.   This had been rendered possible by the disappearance of Russia as a belligerent on the side of the Allies.   Early in December, 1917, orders had been issued " having for their object immediate preparation to meet a strong and sustained hostile offensive."   " In other words," as Sir Douglas Haig stated in his dispatch, " a defensive policy was adopted, and all necessary arrangements, as complete as the time and troops available could make them, were adopted."

As February gave way to March, all indications, most cleverly accumulated by our Intelligence Department, pointed to the fact that the Germans intended to attack in force on the Arras-St. Quentin front, and that the date would be March 20th or 21st.   All troops had accordingly been warned.   All batteries, including 94, had selected reserve positions, to which they could withdraw if necessary.   Reserve lines of trenches had been dug by the infantry, or been marked out.   The artillery had special ''counter-preparation '' programmes and targets allotted, which ensured that fire could be brought at any moment of the

day or night on all likely places of assembly and
trenches whence the enemy could debouch.
" Battle stations " had been detailed for all
units, and could be manned at any time without
delay.

The personnel of 94 had been instructed in
these general considerations. For the week prior
to March 21st it expended many rounds of
harassing fire, chiefly by night, on its counter-
preparation targets. The general feeling among
the troops was, however, one of confidence that
the measures and precautions taken would suffice
to foil any attack.

When, therefore, at 4.30 a.m. on March 21st,
a roar of German guns broke out, accompanied by
the " phee-ut " of gas-shells bursting in the
position, every man in 94 realised that " der
Tag " had at last dawned. Unfortunately a thick
mist shrouded the ground, rendering all observation impossible. The pre-arranged schemes of
lamp and flag communication broke down. Telephone lines were cut at once by the shelling, but
fire was immediately opened, without orders, on
the pre-arranged targets.

Lieuts. Somerville and Hoggan thereupon left
to reconnoitre the position in the front lines.
The gun detachments were subjected to considerable gas and H.E. shelling, but continued
to serve their guns without intermission. About
11 a.m. accounts received from wounded and
stragglers indicated that all was not well in front,
and that the Germans had penetrated our lines,
and were advancing. At noon this was confirmed
by the report from Lieut. Somerville, who had
returned with difficulty owing to the fog, the gas,
and the confused situation. The Germans, it
appeared, had broken our front, had captured
Templeux and Hargicourt, and were still coming
on, meeting with little opposition.

THE FIRST WITHDRAWAL. At 12.30 p.m. orders were received from Brigade Headquarters to prepare to retire, and at 2 p.m. word came to dismount and pull out as soon as possible. 2nd Lieut. J. F. C. Reynolds, R.A.S.C., at this time the Column Officer, succeeded in bringing up four lorries and one caterpillar per gun. The detachments under the Nos. 1, Sgts. F. Harrison, E. Carter, R. Trueman, J. T. Brignall, J. Aird, and W. Jackson, behaved according to the best traditions of the service, and by 7 p.m. the Right and Left Sections were on the road towards their reserve position at Roisel, in spite of fire from German field and machine guns.

During the operation of withdrawal, the Right and Centre Sections came under direct observation of the enemy, parties of whom could be seen on Fervaque Farm ridge, a few hundred yards away, while masses of them were noticed forming up on the slopes between Templeux and Ronssoy. A field gun opened an accurate fire on the Right Section, while the last few stores were being loaded up, and the Major ordered the detachments and lorries to be withdrawn, abandoning the firing beams. These were, however, recovered during the course of the night by a party of volunteers from the section, of whom B.S.M. Finch was one, under Lieut. Clarke. The Left Section lorries could not be brought up nearer than 600 yards to their position. The detachments, however, worked steadily on under Lieut. Somerville till evening. Fortunately for them, the folds of the ground hid them from view of the enemy and they succeeded in bringing everything away.

The Centre Section, which was heavily shelled all day, followed only two hours later, thanks to the cheery example set by Lieut. Lovegrove, the Section Commander. Only one bed-plate, which

had been damaged by shell-fire, two sets of firing
beams, and some stores had to be abandoned.
This was in great measure due to the excellent
work of the caterpillar and lorry drivers under
Sgt. P. W. Smith. During that night the latter
made a most gallant attempt to save some 6-inch
howitzers east of Hesbecourt, but was driven back
by machine-gun fire, losing one caterpillar.

A BATTLE OF
MOVEMENT.
While it is easy to recall to those
present the incidents of this and the
succeeding days of the retreat, it
would be difficult to convey to the lay reader any
adequate idea of what actually took place. At
the will of the enemy, the orderly conditions of
static warfare had given way, in one instant, to a
battle of movement. The cut and dried routine
of previous months suddenly gave place, without
warning, to individual initiative and resource.
Information as to the position of our troops at
any time was, by the nature of the case, extremely
difficult to obtain and often unreliable. All
units and formations moved from point to point
so rapidly as to make their location often obscure.
From the nature of the situation, orders were often
slow to formulate, hard to communicate, and
difficult to execute. All movement was hampered
by an abnormal congestion of road traffic, which
had to be seen to be believed. And above all, there
was the ever-present threat of the oncoming enemy.

The 9·2-inch howitzer is not an easy weapon to
handle under these conditions. No man who
has not served with this calibre can have any
adequate notion of the amount of labour involved
in mounting and dismounting this weighty equipment under all conditions in the field, least of all
when under pressure from the enemy, and when
deliberate methods and pre-arranged plans of
necessity give place to a policy of *ad hoc*. The
narrative of the succeeding days of the retreat, as

it affected 94, should be interpreted in the light of these reflections.

On the night of March 21st, the MARCH 22ND. Battery, as has been seen, was concentrated at Roisel with the intention of covering the defence of our " Brown Line," a system of half-dug trenches running through the positions which had just been vacated. But on the morning of the 22nd the Germans, again aided by the mist which was very thick till mid-day, had broken through that line at 8 a.m., by which time they were only a few hundred yards east of the village, which, however, they did not enter until shortly after 11 a.m. The Battery received orders to retire with the utmost despatch to Cartigny, and select a position for the defence of our last, or " Green Line." Owing to a breakdown, a number of stores, a second caterpillar, with one carriage and bed-plate, had here to be abandoned before starting, though previously rendered unserviceable to the enemy. On arriving at Cartigny, word came to proceed southwest to Mons-en-Chaussée, a village about four miles east of the Somme, and there put four guns into action. That place was reached at 8 p.m., and work on the gun-pits was immediately begun.

In the meantime Major Sandford, after having ensured the safe withdrawal of the guns, stayed behind in Roisel to the last moment. He was able to report to Corps H.A. Headquarters valuable information as to the location and strength of our troops, and the position of the Germans. Detachments of our cavalry, who were now arriving, were also able to profit by his information in deciding on their movements.

At 10 p.m. fresh orders came WEST OF THE from the 23rd Brigade to the effect SOMME. that all the heavy artillery, and all troops other than infantry, certain brigades of field artillery, and a few tanks were to be west of the Somme by dawn on the 23rd.

The road was once more taken, and the Somme crossed at the bridge-head of Brie, where the Engineers were busy mining both bridges to be ready for demolition. A halt was called at 4 a.m. at Villers Carbonnel to enable the men to snatch a few hours' sleep. Their dormitories that night consisted of the Nissen huts which but lately had sheltered the staff of the Fifth Army.

After three hours' sleep, work was commenced on March 23rd on a position selected for the defence of the Brie bridge-head. Bodily fatigue was forgotten in the exhilaration of action, and the gunners buckled to with a will. But shortly afterwards word arrived to withdraw to Estrées, which equally commanded the bridges on the Somme, though at a safer distance.

The journey thither was memorable for the fact that the lorries had first to be turned round on a road crammed with traffic. In order to avoid blocking the road, the guns were diverted into a field and turned there, during which manœuvre they were spotted by a flight of about a dozen German aeroplanes. Circling low overhead, the airmen emptied their machine guns into the Battery, luckily without result. The lorries, taking advantage of a break in the traffic, were reversed on the road. The difficult cross-roads at Villers Carbonnel, through which a dense conflux of transport was passing, and which were being heavily shelled by the Germans, had then to be negotiated. To add to the natural anxieties of the O.C., Cpl. H. C. Smith's caterpillar broke down at this juncture. With great coolness that N.C.O. repaired the machine under fire, an act which earned him his Military Medal. After many other incidents, which can only arise from the congested roads over which a military retirement on a vast scale is being involuntarily conducted, Estrées, a village on the main Brie-Amiens road, was reached about 6 p.m.

THE DEFENCE
OF THE SOMME
BRIDGE-HEAD.
By midnight a gun had here been mounted by Lieut. Somerville with a party of volunteers from all sections, and by 1 a.m. the gunners had the satisfaction of being able to pound away on the east side of the Somme in defence of the important bridges at Brie.

Rumours were current on that morning that the Germans had forced the passage of the river, and by 11.30 a.m. this was confirmed. At noon orders came to cease fire and dismount, and in three hours' time the Battery was once more moving westward towards Foucaucourt.

The night of March 24th saw **94** again digging in a position which had been selected at Rainecourt, but at midnight word came to cease work and be ready to move at 9 a.m. the following morning to Wiencourt to rest and reorganise. The mental and physical strain under which all ranks had been working can readily be imagined. On the way to Wiencourt a complete 9·2-inch howitzer was collected from the Army Heavy Workshops at La Flaque, and deficiencies in this respect thus made good. In fact, **94** now boasted seven " pieces " instead of its complement of six.

A FURTHER
WITHDRAWAL.
The next twenty-four hours were spent in re-sorting stores, which by this time were necessarily in a state of hopeless confusion, and snatching a few hours' sleep. On the following day, the 26th, an alarming report arrived, to the effect that German cavalry had broken through at Caix—at the head of the river Luce—and that the Battery was to go into action at once at Marcelcave, and open fire on the roads in the valley of that river. It appeared that a large gap in our line had been

made, and that the Germans were advancing
rapidly. The choice of position was subsequently
altered, and the Battery sent back to Villers
Bretonneux, which was reached in the afternoon.
A position was selected in the valley west of that
village, where by 6.30 p.m. four platforms had
been laid and two guns half mounted—a magnificent piece of work on the part of the detachments.

BACKWARDS
AND
FORWARDS.
Then came the inspiriting message
from Gen. Foch — now General-
issimo of the Allied Forces—that the
Fifth Army " would not retire
another foot, but fight where it stood to the last
man and the last gun." Gen. C. G. Pritchard,
D.S.O., commanding XIX. Corps Heavy Artillery,
issued orders accordingly, and 94 was even told
to advance to Bayonvillers. Major Sandford
immediately went ahead to select a position, while
the gunners dismounted the guns amid cheers and
reloaded their stores. Owing to the efforts of
Lieuts. Somerville and Lovegrove, who toiled
unremittingly throughout the night with their
men, three guns were ready for action in the
position by 6 a.m. on the morning of the 27th,
and immediately opened fire on likely places of
assembly in the enemy lines. Calls from the
air, and S.O.S. calls from our infantry, were also
promptly answered.

THE LINE
BROKEN.
Meanwhile Lieut. Somerville, in-
defatigable as ever, was observing
from Bayonvillers Church steeple,
and reported that our men were again retiring.
By noon this was confirmed on all sides, and the
Brigade sent a message to dismount at once. By
3 p.m. the Battery was on the road back once
more, and withdrew to the position behind Villers
Bretonneux which it had vacated the previous
night. Remounting was at once proceeded with,
but by 9 p.m. orders were given to " stand easy,"

the intention being to give the men a short rest. At midnight however the situation was judged to be too critical to allow of delay, and word was received to complete mounting as soon as possible. The men were turned out at once, and the two guns were in action by 8 a.m. on the 28th. During that day 100 rounds were fired, and another gun was pulled into a position immediately north of Petit Blangy.

Towards evening, however, it became evident that our infantry were thoroughly disorganised, stragglers were increasing in numbers, and there seemed a possibility that Villers Bretonneux, and the surrounding heights commanding a view of Amiens would fall before dawn. Later that night word came through that the infantry line on the immediate front seemed to have disappeared altogether, and that the eastern outskirts of the village were only held by a band of stragglers from various units and sundry details. The Battery was at once sent farther back—this time to Boves, about six miles south-east of Amiens, which was reached at 5.30 a.m. on the 29th.

THE GERMANS HELD. By this time the personnel was showing not unnatural signs of exhaustion. The urgency of the situation had alone been supplying the stimulus normally afforded by sleep. But rest there was none. By noon on the same day news reached them that the immortal force of odds and ends, subsequently known as " Carey's Force," had, under the personal direction of Brig.-Gen. S. Carey, done valiant work at Villers Bretonneux that night, and successfully filled the gap in the line. 94 was accordingly ordered to trek back in support. At 1 p.m. the Battery started on the journey, and two guns were sited in the Bois l'Abbé, about 2,500 yards west of Villers Bretonneux, the same day. On the 30th they were reported in action, and lines were laid to an O.P. in the church spire of that village, which was subsequently used every day for controlling fire.

THE AUSTRALIANS AT VILLERS BRETONNEUX.

On April 4th the Germans made their second big attack on the village with a view to securing observation on Amiens. They failed, owing to the magnificent fighting of the Australians, supported by British cavalry, who by this time had been hurried up for the defence of Amiens.

The Battery's observation parties, under Capt. Lush and Lieuts. Lovegrove and Hoggan, had a very rough day of it, but succeeded in keeping Headquarters well informed as to the progress of the battle on both sides of Villers Bretonneux. Capt. Lush, who, after nearly two years of this work, was now a seasoned hand at it, looked upon that day as one of his roughest experiences. He described the Germans as being mown down in waves by our artillery fire.

By the end of the day, however, the Germans had penetrated into the outskirts of the village, and 94 was ordered to retire to a position $2\frac{1}{2}$ miles farther back near the cross-roads at Blangy, where Lieut. Somerville had already mounted a gun. Another gun was here dug in on the south side of the main Amiens road. Heavy firing was kept up until April 13th, when the section and stores were handed over *in situ* to 265 Siege Battery.

A REST.

Fully realising the extraordinarily heavy strain to which the personnel of batteries had lately been subjected, the Corps Commander was arranging for their withdrawal by brigades for a rest and refit. 94 was, accordingly, sent to Huppy, near Abbeville, for three weeks. The first few days were spent in making good the arrears of sleep, after

GERMAN 77-MM. FIELD GUN CAPTURED ON AUGUST 26TH, 1918, NEAR MARICOURT.
Used against the enemy by Capt. R. A. E. Somerville, M.C., M.M. It has been presented to the town of Sunderland.

which attention was paid to sorting stores and indenting for deficiencies. A full programme of sight-seeing, swimming, football, and other sports was also arranged. The Battery, headed by Cpl. W. S. Brice, was easily first in the cross-country race organised by the 23rd Brigade.

With this rest ended the " Retreat " for 94. During those three preceding weeks the Battery had moved 85 miles on the road, prepared thirteen positions, in nine of which fire had been opened—and expended over 1500 rounds. The story would be incomplete without a word of well-earned praise for the gallant and tireless efforts of the caterpillar and lorry drivers throughout those anxious days. It seems impossible adequately to convey their sense of devotion to their duties, and their unfailing readiness to back up their brother gunners, as far as lay in their power. 2nd Lieut. Reynolds subsequently received the M.C. for his gallantry.

Casualties had happily been light. CASUALTIES. In addition to several wounded cases, Gr. J. E. Oliver had been killed on his gun, March 21st, and Gr. W. T. Gaston, April 5th. On April 11th, Lieut. Lovegrove earned his third wound stripe. Two bombs had been dropped by enemy airmen, which had " bracketted " the Officers' Mess tent, and a splinter from one entered his shoulder, severely wounding him, and he had to be invalided to England. His loss was very keenly felt. His place was taken by 2nd Lieut. C. Storer, posted to the Battery on April 24th.

E

CHAPTER VIII

PERIOD OF RECOVERY

RESUMPTION OF BRITISH OFFENSIVE

MAY—AUGUST, 1918

IN ACTION AGAIN. By May 1st the batteries of the 23rd Brigade had completed their refitting, and received orders to return to the firing line. They now found themselves with the Australian Corps (Third Army) and were sent to the Albert Sector on the Ancre. On May 3rd the two guns of 94's Left Section were mounted on the western edge of Bresle Wood, while the Right Section dug in on the north-eastern outskirts of Franvillers. The Centre Section was kept on wheels at Baizieux.

INCREASING CONFIDENCE. By this time many factors were contributing to a restoration of the optimism which had been somewhat rudely shaken by the retirement of March.

The new unity of command had completely justified itself by the crushing repulses inflicted on the Germans before Amiens, in April, and in Flanders later in the same month.

There was also the cheering knowledge that our losses both in men and guns had been more than completely replaced, and that all demands for material had been rapidly met.

Moreover, each succeeding week strengthened the opinion that the enemy had staked all his chances of success against the British in one gigantic final throw, which had failed. It seemed, therefore, only a question of time before a British offensive would be resumed, and, with the aid of the American forces now arriving in large numbers, carried to the victorious conclusion which had never been doubted by the British soldier.

As May advanced and the Amiens front solidified, giving no further cause for concern, the heavy guns—which had for some time been echeloned in unusual and considerable depth as a precautionary measure, the better to deal with any further break-through attempt on the part of the enemy—were once more sent forward.

ARTILLERY ACTIVITY. The months of May, June and July on the Somme were accordingly devoted to a vigorous harassing, destructive, and counter-battery fire. The latter had indeed always been a marked feature of the employment of our " Heavies." Both in the localisation and neutralisation of hostile batteries, our organisation had proved itself to be immensely superior to that of the Germans, and accounted, as the latter admitted in confidential documents, for the destruction of a large number of their guns.

During these summer months the aeroplane and balloon were much used by the Battery to obtain observation, while calibration was effected with the aid of triple-line observation by the Field Survey Battalion. A constant watch over the enemy was also maintained by the Battery F.O.O.'s, and many and useful were the reports from " Ducks " and " Drakes," the Battery O.P.'s on the north and west banks of the River Ancre. Sig./Cpl. W. H. Lee (then Sig./Bdr.) and Grs. C. Francis and H. Barker did very good work here as observers.

POSTINGS AND CASUALTIES. In the meantime many changes in personnel had taken place. On May 10th Capt. Lush was appointed Staff-Captain to the C.B.S.O.,

III. Corps, and left the Battery, to the common
regret, after two years' continuous service with it
in the field.   The vacancy was filled by the transfer of Capt. W. L. Opie, from 211 Siege Battery,
a few days later. 2nd Lieut. L. S. Mason was
posted to the Anti-Aircraft Defence Corps, Fourth
Army, on May 18th, and 2nd Lieut. Gardiner
to 5th Field Survey Company on May 30th.
Their places were filled by the arrival of 2nd
Lieuts. R. Hill and G. K. Betts from England,
on May 29th.   Another addition was that of
2nd Lieut. C. R. Selous-Jones, who was transferred from 327 Siege Battery on May 10th.
This officer, however, did not remain long on the
Battery strength.   Whilst acting as F.O.O. on
the night of June 1st–2nd at " Rib " O.P. he
was badly gassed and subsequently invalided
home.

On May 24th Gr. C. H. Schnaar was killed in
the Right Section position at Franvillers by a
shell which struck his dug-out.   Another casualty
was caused by the enemy's night bombing activi-
ties.   On the night May 27th–28th, a hostile
aeroplane bombed Bresle Wood.   Gr. H. Banfield
was killed, and Gr. F. J. Green wounded by one of
the bombs.

During June the influenza epidemic, then raging,
spread to the Battery and affected about thirty
N.C.O.'s and men.   Fortunately they soon recovered and were sent down to the Fourth Army
Rest Camp at Le Treport, under 2nd Lieut. Storer,
for a short convalescent holiday by the sea.

CAPTURE OF VILLE-SUR-ANCRE.   As evidence of our increasing
strength, and in pursuance of the
offensive policy which had now been
initiated, the 2nd Australian Division,
on May 19th, attacked and captured the village of
Ville-sur-Ancre.   94 supported this operation
by neutralising hostile batteries.

CAPTURE OF HAMEL. Harassing tactics were continued, and the Germans were subjected to heavy fire, night raids, and attacks on trenches and positions of local tactical value. An operation of a rather more ambitious nature was the capture on July 4th, by the Australian Corps, in which American troops for the first time in this area participated, of the village of Hamel, on the south bank of the Somme. This attack was really intended to secure important " jumping-off " places for the major operations to follow. Its success was complete, and was generally regarded at the time as a model of the co-operation of all arms.

In order to increase its effective range, the Right Section, on July 12th, was moved up to join the Centre at Ribemont. Shortly afterwards the Battery passed from the Australian Corps to III. Corps Heavy Artillery (Brig.-Gen. A. E. J. Perkins, C.B., C.M.G.). This change involved an alteration of position. On July 20th the two sections at Ribemont were moved into Henencourt and Baizieux respectively, occupying positions on the outskirts of these villages. A few days later Bresle Wood position was evacuated, and the guns there moved to a valley about 1,500 yards north-east of Franvillers. As the Baizieux position was a silent one the Battery personnel was moved round from one section to another, each section in turn thus enjoying a brief spell of rest at the silent position.

On July 12th Lieut. C. Watts had been posted to the Battery from England.

PREPARATIONS FOR THE GREAT OFFENSIVE. Meanwhile the enemy was launching violent attacks against the French in the Champagne and Aisne sectors with considerable success. In doing so, however, he had used up about fifty of his divisions, and the hour was approaching when Marshal Foch had decided to strike back.

The assault on the Somme front was fixed for August 8th—a memorable day in British history. The better to support the attack, guns were pushed well forward. On August 5th the Centre and Left Sections were got ready for action in an advanced position in the village of Ribemont, while the Right was moved to a point about 2,000 yards north of Buire, on the south side of the Albert-Amiens road.

In order to be in a position to exploit any rapid advances, mobile sub-groups of 6-inch howitzer and 60-pounder batteries had been formed. The command of one of these was given to Major Sandford, who was thus detached from 94 on August 4th. The duties of B.C. now devolved on Capt. Opie, who, however, only acted in this capacity for two days, being invalided on the 6th through sickness. Lieut. Somerville was accordingly appointed Captain and took command.

INITIAL SUCCESS. The main attack on the Amiens front was south of the Somme. The function of the III. Corps—which lay on the north of that river, and formed the left flank of the Fourth Army—was to align their front with any advance on the south. The success of our arms in conjunction with our French Allies was most marked. The German lines were pierced and penetrated to a depth of many miles. A feature of the advance was the way in which the armoured cars, whippet tanks, cavalry, and mobile guns supported the initial efforts of the infantry.

FORWARD MOVES. In consequence of this success the artillery was at once sent further forward. The Centre and Left Sections accordingly, on August 11th, moved from Ribemont into Ville-sur-Ancre, where the ruined condition of the village lent itself admirably to

effective concealment of the guns. After ten days'
heavy firing in this position the Centre Section,
on August 23rd, was sent forward to Dernancourt,
while a day later the Right Section advanced to
Meaulte. Not a round, however, was fired from
the latter, as the enemy had been driven out of
range before mounting could be completed.

The advance of the III. Corps front had now
become more rapid and the consequent congestion
of roads, with the excessive strain on motor
transport, rendered impossible the employment of
all heavy artillery. 94 accordingly received
orders to concentrate at Meaulte, where guns and
equipment were overhauled. Some of the officers
and men were now lent as reinforcements to other
batteries of the Brigade, which, being of lighter
calibre and consequently more mobile, were
remaining in touch with the enemy.

As far as the Battery was concerned, the first
stage of the advance was thus ended. The arduous work involved by the rapid moves had been
cheerfully and gallantly performed. Sig./Bdr.
W. M. Dakers (North Scottish R.G.A.) was awarded
the French " Médaille d'Honneur (avec glaives en
bronze) " for his excellent work on the lines.

TRANSFER
OF MAJ.
SANDFORD.
On August 31st Major Sandford,
whose sub-group had now been dis-
persed, was transferred to command
355 Siege Battery, one of the 6-inch
howitzer batteries of the Brigade.*

CAPTURE OF
GERMAN
GUNS.
It is interesting to record here
how two German 77-mm. guns
passed into the possession of the
Battery about this time. Capt.
Somerville, when acting as F.O.O. for the Brigade
near Maricourt during the last days of August, dis-
covered two 77-mm. guns that had been hurriedly

* Lieut. W. R. Clarke was posted to III. Corps H.A. on September 5th.

abandoned by the enemy without being put out
of action. Observing hostile movement near
Curlu, he, with the assistance of his telephonists,
Cpl. W. S. Brice and Sig. W. H. Anderson, turned
one gun round and fired over 100 rounds into
the enemy. For this act Capt. Somerville was
awarded a bar to his M.C.

These guns were subsequently allotted to the
Battery as captured trophies. They are now in
the custody of the Durham R.G.A. (T.) and the
town of Sunderland respectively, as an acknow-
ledgment of the largely territorial character of the
original personnel of 94.

CHAPTER IX

The Great Advance

SEPTEMBER—NOVEMBER, 1918

A NEW
C.O.

The command of the Battery was
now given to Major Charles E.
Berkeley Lowe, M.C.,* North Scottish
R.G.A. (T.), who had been serving in a sister
9·2-inch Howitzer Battery (143 Siege) since December, 1916, and had previously served in France
as a private in the infantry (" London Scottish ")
for thirteen months during 1914–15. It was a curious coincidence that while 94's old Sgt.-Maj.—
B.S.M. Cook—after being invalided home in
October, 1916, was subsequently posted as B.S.M.
to 143 Siege, that battery was now to furnish
a Major for 94. It will also be remembered
that 94 and 143 exchanged equipments in
August, 1916.

---

* Subsequently awarded D.S.O.

The new O.C. found the Battery
on September 8th resting at Meaulte,
the little village, now totally destroyed, about one mile south of Albert. Next
day he received orders to move up to Templeux-
la-Fosse, where Brigade Headquarters had been
installed.

After arrival there, in advance of the lorry and
gun columns, positions for the guns were immediately reconnoitred near Villers-Faucon—a village
in name only, for it had borne the treble shock
of the pre-March, 1918, stationary warfare, the
German attack in March, and our recapture in
September.

In pursuance of the general tactical policy at
this time of almost daily advances, gun positions
had to be selected well forward in order to be able
successfully to support subsequent progress. It
was therefore no uncommon thing—rather the
reverse—to find the stately 9·2-inch howitzers
within 1,500 or 2,000 yards of the enemy lines,
and firing alongside their brethren of the "Field."

Positions were accordingly found that same
day—four guns immediately west of the village,
and one section in front of it behind the railway
embankment, about 200 yards south of the Villers
Faucon-Ronssoy road, positions which—in view
of the general scarcity of flash cover, and the
number of guns that had accordingly to be sited
in limited areas—the Battery was distinctly lucky
to secure.

At 5 p.m. on that day, orders were received to
pull the forward section into action the same
night. Personnel and stores, which had by this
time arrived, were accordingly sent on to prepare
the gun-pits—under Lieut. G. C. L. Chamberlain,
in the absence of Lieut. C. Watts, the Left Section
commander—notwithstanding that sub-sections,
owing to detached details, were at half strength,

and that a long day's work had already been done.

THE CATERPILLAR SECTION'S FEAT. The real question was—would the caterpillars and guns which had started from Meaulte at 8 a.m. the same morning be able to cover the distance of over twenty miles *per saltum*, and, if so, would the drivers and machines be physically capable of completing the remaining four miles to the gun positions and then—work being forbidden by daylight—help to pull in the loads before dawn ?

About 8 p.m. Sgt. R. Burslem, the caterpillar Sergeant, who was generally recognised as being second to none of his kind in France, arrived at Templeux-la-Fosse and announced that his six loads were approaching. No man who has not done twelve hours' travelling and driving in a caterpillar, covered over twenty miles on a hot day, and been faced with all the vexatious delays incidental to such journeys, will appreciate the nature of this feat. Being told that two guns were to continue the journey forthwith, Sgt. Burslem, nevertheless, insisted on guiding them up himself, and found the drivers—as ever—game for anything. So away they snorted after a short break, arriving at the position near midnight.

Owing to heavy bursts of high explosive and gas shell—during which Sgt. J. Aird of No. 5 Sub-Section was wounded—the heaviness of the ground from rain, the shortage of men, and the inkiness of the night, the work of mounting was greatly delayed, and at 6 a.m., when daylight forced the party to break off, was not quite complete.

THE GENERAL'S ASTONISH-MENT. It subsequently appeared that the order to mount this section on the same day as the journey from Meaulte had rested on a verbal misunderstanding. When Brig.-Gen. Perkins (III. Corps H.A.) was told next morning that 94's two forward guns were partly mounted 1,500 yards from the enemy, and would certainly be ready for action before the following dawn, he expressed his surprise at the performance and complimented the Battery on it.

A few days later the remaining four guns were all mounted in one night in the other position immediately west of Villers Faucon, and reported ready for action by 9 a.m. the following morning —a most satisfactory performance on the part of the Nos. 1 concerned, Sgt. F. Harrison, M.M. (No. 1), Sgt. W. Bate (No. 2), Sgt. R. Trueman (No. 3), Sgt. J. T. Brignall, M.S.M. (No. 4)—the big four—who, among other difficulties, had to contend with an execrable approach.

CASUALTIES. In spite of heavy bursts of shelling, including gas—to which both sections, but more especially the forward, were subject—the casualties in this position were remarkably light. The Hun had a curious knack of setting No. 1's cartridges ablaze, but more were always forthcoming. One night, too, a shell struck the shattered roof of a shanty in which a dozen or more men were sleeping. By a miracle it only wounded four, Bdr. F. Bennett, Gr. R. W. Moore, Gr. F. E. Robinson, and Gr. E. Nelson. Sgt. E. Carter, now in charge of the Signal Section, was severely shaken and stunned, but he refused to be relieved from his duties, to the execution of which he clung throughout the night and following day with an exemplary devotion. B.S.M. F. C. Finch and Sgt. Harrison distinguished themselves as usual by binding up and evacuating the wounded, and generally showing magnificent examples of coolness and steadiness under fire.

On another occasion Sgt. Harrison and his detachment were in action on their gun, when a shell burst three yards away, luckily without hitting anyone, though for a moment scattering the detachment. Sgt. Harrison, however, instantly stepped on to the firing platform and pulled the lanyard, firing the gun, which restored confidence all round. It was this incident, among others, which helped to earn him his richly deserved Military Medal.

BATTLES. From these positions, and one slightly forward on the St. Emilie-Roisel Road—which was subsequently selected, as the attack progressed, for Lieut. (then 2nd Lieut.) E. S. Hopkins's Centre Section—the Battery during September supported the attacks which gained for us the general line Hargicourt-E. of Ronssoy-Lempire.

During these operations, Lieut. (then 2nd Lieut.) G. C. L. Chamberlain did some very good reconnaissance work, laying and maintaining long lengths of cable, ascertaining the progress of our troops during the attack, and sending back valuable information by wire, lamp, flag and runner. Sig./Cpl. H. Lee (then Sig./Bdr.) distinguished himself by his gallantry and good work when out with Lieut. Chamberlain on these occasions.

Further attacks having been contemplated by the Higher Command with a view to flinging the Germans back on their much-advertised Hindenburg Line, and subsequently breaking through that, orders were received to push up all guns as far as possible. The days were over when Battery Commanders could reconnoitre and select positions naturally suited for their guns in respect of concealment and accessibility, while at the same time satisfying tactical requirements. A Brigade Commander might be told to site his force in a certain area or map - square. Half - a - dozen batteries would accordingly be crowded into the allotted space as best they might.

Thus was it here. The village
RONSSOY. of Ronssoy had an unenviable reputation at this time as the especial
object of German hatred and " strafing." It
was constantly shelled with H.E. and gas. There
was not a house intact in the whole village, and
the ground was everywhere pitted and pocked
with craters and shell holes—souvenirs of three
years of war. This made the passage of heavy
guns doubly difficult, and restricted immeasurably
the number of possible sites. The configuration
of the ground, too, further reduced the number of
gun positions, for, being on the 140 metre con-
tour, it was overlooked from the high ground to the
north which formed the eastern bank of the St.
Quentin Canal, where the Hindenburg Line at
this part was sited. As if to increase the tortures
of the Battery Commander in search of positions
here, orders had been received from the Heavy
Artillery of the Australian Corps, to which the
Battery was now transferred, that no guns would
be allowed to fire across roads within 100 yards of
them.

Notwithstanding these difficulties and draw-
backs, the six guns were eventually crammed
with all possible haste among the most westerly
ruins of the village, on either side of the Epehy-
Ronssoy road.

PREPARING   All work had to be done at night
FOR ACTION.   in order to deny to the enemy any
indications of a further impending
attack. Cpl. C. Harrington, R.A.S.C., then in
charge of the caterpillars, displayed great gallantry and determination in bringing the guns up
under gas and H.E. shell over an execrable cross-
country track on pitch dark nights. Sgt. A. H.
Birks, D.C.M. (then Cpl.), No. 3 Sub-Section, and
Cpls. R. Smith and A. T. Webb (No. 4 Sub-
Section) distinguished themselves by pulling their

respective guns out from their previous positions
where they had been firing heavily until 7 p.m.,
and remounting them at Ronssoy the same night—
so that by far the greater part of the work was
completed by dawn in spite of intermittent gusts
of shelling—a feat which only a 9·2-inch gunner
will fully appreciate.

CAPTURE OF
HINDENBURG
LINE.
In this position the Battery helped
to pave the way for and supported
the successful attacks made in this
area during the last days of September and first of October by British, Australian
and American troops, which resulted in the
breaching of the Hindenburg Line, and enabled
our armies to sweep onward to yet greater
victories.

CASUALTIES.
The Battery's casualties were,
however, regrettably heavy. Subjected night and day to heavy and
accurate harassing fire and concentrations, the
losses amounted to one killed (died of wounds),
Gr. J. W. Seargent, and twenty wounded (including
Sgt. Carter). No. 3 Sub-Section suffered the
most. During an especially heavy three-minute
concentration on the Battery, a 5·9-inch shell fell
just behind their gun, wounding nine, including
Bdr. J. Hudson, Bdr. W. Robinson, and Grs. J.
Costello, A. H. Cove, J. H. Kingdom, and C. W.
Edwards. No. 1 gun bore a more charmed
existence. One shell hit its earth-box, rendering it useless, while another penetrated below its
rear firing beam, but happily failed to explode.
In consequence of this the gun became one of the
chief side-shows in Ronssoy for the curious visitor.

Gr. G. Braybrook also came into prominence
by his stout-heartedness, cheerfulness, and great
gallantry when his cookhouse (with its precious
contents) was repeatedly hit, and at last totally
destroyed—he himself escaping as if by a miracle.

The detachments showed the most praise-
worthy steadiness under these trying conditions
and by their good work further enhanced the
reputation of the Battery. B.S.M. Finch, as
usual, was to the fore in rendering first-aid to
wounded and organising stretcher parties.* Bdr.
D. Hooper (then Gr.), No. 3 Sub-Section, distinguished himself by his untiring energy and
great gallantry while mounting and serving his
gun. Cpl. P. Hanlon, as the No. 1 of No. 5 gun,
infused the greatest confidence into his detachment by his indifference and coolness under shell-
fire—actions which contributed to his subsequent
earning of the Military Medal.

Mention must also be made of Sig./Cpl. (then
Sig./Bdr.) W. Davies, who, in the absence of his
Officer and Sergeant (both in hospital), " carried
on " in charge of the Signalling Section, and was
personally and directly responsible that communications—both forward and rear—which were
being continually cut night and day, were always
so rapidly and effectively re-established in the
face of great danger.

WORK OF THE
BATTERY
COLUMN.
One of the greatest difficulties of
this position was the supply of
ammunition, which had to be
brought from a great distance by
motor lorries and could only arrive at night over
execrable roads which were both heavily shelled
and choked with traffic. This threw a great
strain upon drivers, many of whom, at this time,
got no rest for successive days and nights. But
the urgency of the tactical situation, which each
man instinctively appreciated, infused a common
motive force into drivers and gunners alike; and
work which in peace time, or on manœuvres,
would never have been deemed practicable, was

---

* B.S.M. Finch was subsequently awarded the D.C.M. for his
gallantry on this and other occasions.

now cheerfully undertaken and gallantly accomplished.

It was at this time, too, that the personality of the new Column Officer, who, like many of his predecessors, had come with a great mechanical experience at his back, which was always reflected in the condition of the Battery lorries—Lieut. T. V. Harrison, R.A.S.C. (M.T.)—began to make itself felt in further promoting and fostering good feeling and a common *esprit de corps* between the Battery and its Ammunition Column.

94 DROPS OUT. With the breaching of the Hindenburg Line, the British advance assumed a yet more open and mobile character, rendering the employment of all batteries impossible, owing to the limitations of roads, ammunition supply and transport. The strain on lorries had lately been intense, and the percentage of breakdowns had of necessity risen alarmingly, while at the same time workshops had either been left too far back to be fully effective in coping with this congestion of casualties, or were actually engaged in bringing their own shops forward to more central sites.

Under these circumstances the 9·2-inch howitzers (Mark I.) were ordered, among others, to stand fast, and 94 accordingly had an interval wherein to survey and take stock of damages due to enemy action, and indent for deficiencies. The Major took this opportunity for initiating a course of infantry drill with a view to further smartening the personnel, sharpening up the discipline, and incidentally breaking in the reinforcements which by this time—thanks to the admirable efficiency of the R.A. Section, 3rd Echelon—were already arriving to replace casualties.

SALVING GERMAN GUNS. Orders were subsequently received to salve as far as possible captured German guns that were

ENLARGEMENT FROM A SNAPSHOT OF NO. 4 GUN IN ACTION AT RONSSOY.
(September, 1918.)

lying over the blasted battle-fields on the banks of the St. Quentin Canal. The gunners looked upon this as a pleasant sport, and with the willing help of the caterpillar men, and a lavish expenditure of petrol, which might have horrified the authorities had they known—collected in the course of a couple of weeks over twenty guns of all calibres up to 5·9-inch, and many machine guns. These were duly dumped at Ronssoy in the " 94 S.B. Jerry Gun Park," as it was styled.

THE GENERAL'S THANKS.   For this, the O.C. received a special letter conveying the thanks of the G.O.C. R.A. XIII. Corps (whose H.A. was commanded by Brig.-Gen. J. D. Sherer, D.S.O., and to which the Battery had by this time been transferred) for its excellent work and the unexpected number of guns it had salved, a letter which was much appreciated by the men.

F.O.O.'S.   During the operations in October, the 23rd Brigade had on several occasions made use of Capt. Somerville's experience and ability in reconnaissance work by sending him forward on battle days to report progress and send back any information of value. Sig./Bdr. Dakers displayed great ability and gallantry when out with Capt. Somerville on these days, in the use of the Lucas lamp and generally in establishing and maintaining communications under the most trying circumstances. The Brigade, at this time under the temporary command of Major Sandford, had a well-deserved reputation for supplying Corps H.A. with early, first-hand, and reliable information on such occasions, and 94 was not seldom the source from which the information came. Subsequently Capt. Somerville was sent for by the Brigade to act as Signal Officer. He remained at those Headquarters until the Battery's transfer to the 47th

F

Brigade. (Lieut.-Col. F. E. Andrewes, D.S.O.) in December.

On another battle day in October—that on which our troops stormed across the River Selle, south of Le Câteau—Major Lowe, when acting as one of the Brigade F.O.O.'s, had the satisfaction of locating a German gun which had been hurriedly pushed up to the high ground east of the river, and was firing on the Church of St. Benin, a village in our lines, whose spire was brought down with the sixth round. The Major quickly engaged the offender with a 6-inch Howitzer Battery,* silencing the gun and putting the detachment to flight.

CAPTURED GUNS TURNED AGAINST THE ENEMY. Reference may also be made to another exploit of interest on October 23rd, near Pommereuil, a village about two miles east of Le Câteau, and situated on the western fringe of the Bois l'Evêque. This latter, extending eastwards to a depth of two miles, formed the final objective of the British attack on that day, starting from a line about 1,000 yards east of Le Câteau.

A small party of three officers and a few gunners—all volunteers from 94, under the command of the Major†—set out before dawn with the object of locating any German batteries that might be over-run in the course of our attack, and turning them against the enemy.

After some delay, the advance of the infantry having been temporarily held up by German machine guns, they entered Pommereuil, and a message was sent back for the lorry with the gunners and stores. That lorry soon had the proud pleasure of being the first to rattle through the village on the heels of the Huns.

---

* 355 Siege Battery.   † The other officers were Lts. Hoggan and Hopkins,

Shortly afterwards a battery of German 77-mm. guns was located 1,000 yards north of the village. The guns were still warm, but had all been put out of action by the Germans before being abandoned. Thanks, however, to the skill and energy of Ftr./Gr. J. Tugby, whose willingness on all occasions was most commendable, a breech block was removed from one and fitted to another. In a very short time over 200 rounds of his own metal, which had been left lying in the gun-pits, was being fired into the retreating enemy, to the boundless joy of the party.

THE LAST. ACTION.   Shortly after this episode the Battery was ordered into action near Bousies, and a position was selected for four guns 1,000 yards north-east of that village and about 1,500 yards from the German lines. All ranks were glad at the prospect, as the gunners said, " of sending a few more pills over to Jerry." The British attack was planned for November 4th, and included the forcing of the Canal de la Sambre at Landrecies and the capture or isolation of the formidable Forêt de Mormal, north of that place. Considerable opposition was expected from these *points d'appui*, and the heavy artillery was accordingly reinforced for the occasion.

After some initial delays, the attack proved eminently successful, and our troops were out of range on the following day—an advance which was subsequently exploited with all possible energy until the signing of the Armistice gave it its final halt on November 11th.

The Battery was very pleased to have had a hand in the closing operation. It fell to No. 4 Sub-Section, under Sgt. Brignall, actually to fire the last round from 94.

All ranks will indeed ever be mindful of the great privilege that fell to them of being able to

"C" Form.

MESSAGES AND SIGNALS.

Army Form C
(In book
No. of Messages

Prefix _AB_ Code _0750_ Words _16_

Received from _Copes_ _HC_

Service Instructions _QN Hy_

Sent, or sent out.

At _____ m.

To _____

By _____

Office Stamp.

Q-11 11 18-1

SIGNALS

Handed in at _____ Office _____ m. Received _0750_ m.

TO | 23 Bde RGA

Sender's Number.	Day of Month.	In reply to Number.	A A A
BM/1233	11 11 18		

Hostilities will cease at
11 00 hours today a a a
Further instructions follow

FROM | _HA_ _0750_
PLACE & TIME |

* This line, except A A A, should be erased, if not required.

Wt. W54/P735. 200,000 Pads. 3/18 H. W. & V., Ld. (E. 2899).

ORIGINAL TELEGRAM ORDERING CESSATION OF HOSTILITIES.
(November 11th, 1918.)

take a part, however humble, in the operations
of the British Army in France, which, after count-
less checks, a colossal expenditure of sustained
and organised effort throughout the entire chain
of command, the use of the most incredible moun-
tains of munitions and war material of every sort
and description, gathered from the uttermost
corners of the earth, together with the undying
devotion to duty and the greatest gallantry in-
variably displayed by all ranks when in action
against the enemy, and which illuminated each
day of four grim years, resulted in the complete
and crushing overthrow of German military power,
and the code of morals for which it stood.

CHAPTER X

DEMOBILISATION

NOVEMBER, 1918—JUNE, 1919

EDUCATION
AND
RECREATION.
After the cessation of active
hostilities, it was evident that some
weeks or months would elapse before
demobilisation—which had been ar-
ranged for by individuals to suit the industrial
needs of the country, and not by units—could
become general. Every effort was accordingly
made to instruct and amuse men during this
interval.

An education scheme was started, and the
Battery officers soon organised classes in Elec-
tricity, Engineering, English, Arithmetic, French,
Shorthand, Book-keeping, and Mathematics—
from which it was believed that many men derived
considerable benefit. Lieut. S. Platt, who had
been posted to the Battery in October, took a

leading part in this work, showing himself no less accomplished as a scholar than he was efficient on the sports field and parade-ground. Football matches, sports, concerts and theatres were everywhere rapidly organised under Battery, Brigade, or Corps auspices.

At the 23rd Brigade sports, held at Hecq in December, 94 carried off all the chief honours of the day (including a most exciting and memorable tug-of-war)—thanks in the main to the successful efforts of Lieut. S. Platt, Bdr. E. F. Pett, Gr. W. Kavanagh and Gr. M. O'Keeffe, a good long-distance runner.

FAREWELL TO 23RD BRIGADE.
The 23rd Brigade, in which the Battery had served since January, 1918, was now under orders to proceed to Germany with the Army of Occupation — less its 9·2-inch Battery. Col. Budgen accordingly said farewell to 94 on parade in a few cordial words of congratulation. All ranks deeply regretted parting with so gallant and able a soldier.

TRANSFER TO 47TH BRIGADE.
The Battery was now transferred to the 47th Brigade (Lt.-Col. F. E. Andrewes, D.S.O.) and proceeded to billets in Beauvois, a village mid-way between Le Câteau and Cambrai. A very memorable and enjoyable Christmas dinner was held in a hall at Le Câteau, at which the "Column" was also present. Thanks to the personal efforts of Lieut. Harrison (R.A.S.C.) and Lieut. Hopkins, this proved a very great success, to which a couple of roasted pigs, fattened up in the Battery and killed for the occasion, with three barrels of beer, doubtless contributed. The feast was followed by a concert, during which a farce in two acts, entitled " Topsy Turvy " (which had been composed by the officers and acted by them) was presented. The expenses of the dinner were entirely defrayed out of the

profits of the Battery canteen, which had for some months been managed with conspicuous energy and success by Lieut. Hopkins, who always took a deep interest in everything concerning the personal comfort of the men.

DEMOBILI-SATION. Early in 1919 men began to dribble away in twos and threes, as allotments for their release came through, and by February the Battery was down to cadre strength (two officers and forty-seven other ranks) plus those who were being retained for the Armies of Occupation. The latter, totalling about sixty, were gradually drafted up to the Rhine in the course of the three following months.

On June 24th the cadre, less an equipment guard of one officer* and fifteen men, who remained to look after the guns, crossed the Channel. On arriving at Dover the men were sent to their respective dispersal areas, and 94 Siege Battery ceased to be.

---

* Lt. Betts.

CHAPTER XI

Nominal Rolls

PART   I.—Roll of Honour.

PART   II.—Honours and Awards (Officers, N.C.O.'s and men).

PART III.—Nominal Roll of Officers.

PART IV.—Nominal Roll of N.C.O.'s and men of original unit, who served with the Battery throughout its fighting in France (May, 1916—November, 1918).

PART   V.—Remainder of original unit (W.O.'s, N.C.O.'s and men).

PART VI.—Reinforcements (W.O.'s, N.C.O.'s and men).

PART VII.—R.A.S.C. (M.T.) (Attached), Officers, N.C.O.'s and men.

PART VIII.—Summary of Battery positions occupied.

N.B. (I.)—" To Hospital, " " Invalided " or " Evacuated to United Kingdom," etc. The majority of casualties thus described must be understood to be wounded cases. A few only were due to sickness.

(II.)—A few men were posted to the Battery after the cessation of hostilities on November 11th, 1918. Their names have **not** been included in these rolls.

ROLL OF HONOUR.*

(1) R.G.A.

REGTL. NO.	NAME.	RANK.	DATE.	PLACE.	NATURE OF DEATH.
5796	FLEWKER, H.	Gnr.	11/7/16		Died from injuries received in railway accident.
69713	THOMSON, A. M.	"	24/8/16	Ovillers	Died of wounds.
6072	ELTRINGHAM, T.	"	27/8/16	"	Killed in action.
56704	McMULLEN, F. J.	Bdr.	27/8/16	"	"
5788	BARR, J. W.	Gnr.	4/9/16	La Boisselle	Died of wounds.
64172	COLLICK, J. H., M.M.	"	14/10/16	"	"
1108	HOLMES, W.	"	20/2/17	Thiepval	Killed in action.
85274	HOLTHAM, W. F.	"	4/4/17	Grandcourt	Died from burns.
348201	MADDOCKS, G. E.	"	26/4/17	Vaulx Vraucourt	Died of wounds.
67283	SMITH, W. H.	"	12/5/17	"	Killed in action.
101277	BALLS, O. H.	"	14/6/17	Le Bizet	"
91637	CAMPBELL, W.	"	18/6/17	"	"
	DE BEER, B. H.	2nd Lt.	10/7/17	Nieuport	"
80092	CASON, F.	Gnr.	10/7/17	"	"
59368	DAY, A. V.	"	10/7/17	"	Died of wounds.
77941	KELLETT, H.	"	10/7/17	"	Killed in action.
32734	COX, A. H.	"	12/7/17	"	"
21431	MASON, J.	Cpl.	13/7/17	"	Died of wounds.
58257	DUCKELS, C. F.	Sgt.	20/7/17	"	Killed in action.
120135	NEWBY, J. A.	Gnr.	15/8/17	"	Died of wounds.

* Arranged in chronological order.

REGTL. NO.	RANK.	NAME.	DATE.	PLACE.	NATURE OF DEATH.
59171	Gnr.	Edwards, J. S.	12/ 8/17	Nieuport	Killed in action.
97750	,,	Ryder, R.	12/ 8/17	,,	,, ,, ,,
130418	,,	Dorrington, W. A.	20/ 8/17	,,	Died of wounds.
87176	F./Gnr.	Freeman, F. T.	16/ 9/17	,,	Killed in action.
337859	W./Gnr.	Mayes, E.	16/ 9/17	,,	,, ,, ,,
49784	Gnr.	Caddick, B.	26/10/17	,,	,, ,, ,,
146485	,,	Wayman, H. O.	29/10/17	,,	Died of wounds.
58905	,,	Edser, G. H.	19/11/17	,,	Killed in action.
33768I	,,	Jenson, H. W.	24/11/17	,,	,, ,, ,,
20059	Sgt.	Collyer, J., M.M.	24/11/17	Roisel	,, ,, ,,
362435	Gnr.	Oliver, J. E.	21/ 3/18	Petit Blangy	Died of wounds.
177495	,,	Gaston, W. J.	5/ 4/18	Franvillers	Killed in action.
109148	,,	Schnaar, C. H.	24/ 5/18	Bresle Wood	,, ,, ,,
98609	,,	Banfield, H.	27/ 5/18	Ronssoy	Died of wounds.
206314	,,	Sargeant, J. W.	7/10/18	Troisvilles	,, ,, ,,
61654	,,	Millen, F. W.	2/11/18		,, ,, ,,
150106	Sig.	Bradbury, G.	7/11/18	Evacuated from Ribemont	Died from influenza.

(2) R.A.S.C. (M.T.) ATTACHED.

REGTL. NO.	RANK.	NAME.	DATE.	PLACE.	NATURE OF DEATH.
170283	Pte.	Sparkes	June, 1916	Bayencourt	Died of wounds.
180334	L.,/Cpl.	Brown, A.	Oct., 1918	Beaurevoir	Killed in action.
		Jones, E. A.	Feb., 1919	Caudry	Died in hospital of pneumonia.

PART II.

HONOURS AND AWARDS.

(1) OFFICERS.

RANK.	NAME.	AWARD.	DATE OF AWARD.	WHERE OBTAINED.
Maj. (since Lieut.-Col.)	Sandford, D. A., D.S.O	Mentions in dispatches.	Jan., 1917 Jan., 1918	} Somme and Nieuport.
		Bar to D.S.O.	June, 1918	March retirement on Somme.
Maj.	Lowe, C. E. B., M.C.	D.S.O.	June, 1919	} Final advance, September–November, 1918.
		Mention in dispatches.	July, 1919	
Capt.	Grant, F.	M.C.	Jan., 1918	Nieuport.
,,	Lush, M. S.	M.C.	Sept., 1916	Somme.
		Bar to M.C.	Nov., 1917	Nieuport.
Capt. (then 2nd Lieut.)	Somerville, R. A. E., M.M.	M.C.	Nov., 1917	,,
		Bar to M.C.	Sept., 1918	Maricourt.
Lieut. (then 2nd Lieut.)	Cassidy, D. M.	M.C.	Sept., 1916	Somme.

REGTL. NO.	RANK.	NAME.	AWARD.	DATE OF AWARD.	WHERE OBTAINED.
358202	B.S.M.	Finch, F. C.	D.C.M.	June, 1919	Final advance, September–November, 1918.
337832	B.Q.M.S. (then Sgt.)	Gilmour, J. H.	M.M.	July, 1917	Nieuport.
337734	Sgt. (then Cpl.)	Birks, A. H.	Belgian Decoration Militaire.	June, 1917	Messines.
33806I	Sgt.	Brignall, J. T.	D.C.M.	Dec., 1918	Ronssoy.
20059	„	*Collyer, J.	M.S.M.	Jan., 1919	Continuous gallant service.
			M.M.	July, 1917	Nieuport.
			Bar to M.M.	Nov., 1917	„
338059	„	Harrison, F.	M.M.	Oct., 1918	Villers Faucon.
58924	„	Toop, A. V.	M.M.	Sept., 1916	Somme.
338056	Cpl.	Brice, W. S.	M.S.M.	June, 1918	Continuous gallant service.
I02795	Sig./Cpl.	Davies, W. H.	Mention in dispatches.	July, 1919	Final British advance.
48999	Cpl. (then Gnr.)	Dodd, J.	M.M.	July, 1917	Nieuport.
I30II	Cpl.	Hanlon, P.	M.M.	Oct., 1918	Ronssoy.
66065	Bdr. (then Gnr.)	Armitage, T.	M.M.	July, 1917	Nieuport.
45600	Bdr.	Cunningham, A.	M.M.	Sept., 1916	Somme.

365645	Bdr. (then L./Bdr.)	Dakers, W. M.	French Medaille d'Honneur.	Aug., 1918	Ribemont.
78317	Bdr.	Edwards, W. S.	M.M.	April, 1918	March retirement on Somme.
338068	Bdr. (then Gnr.)	Rusby, H. R.	M.M.	July, 1917	Nieuport.
68264	L./Bdr. (then Gnr.)	Rose, F. R.	M.M.	July, 1917	,,
64172	Gnr.	*Collick, J. H.	M.M.	Sept., 1916	Somme.
86583	Sig.	Dolby, H.	M.M.	Mar., 1918	Somme.

(3) R.A.S.C. (M.T.) ATTACHED.

167966	Lieut.	Reynolds, J. F. C.	M.C.	May, 1918	March retirement on Somme.
	Cpl.	Smith, H. C.	M.M.	April, 1918	,, ,, ,,

* Since killed or died of wounds.

PART III.

NOMINAL ROLL OF R.G.A. OFFICERS.

(ARRANGED IN CHRONOLOGICAL ORDER.)

RANK.	NAME.	PERIOD WITH UNIT.		HOME ADDRESS.	REMARKS.
		From	To		
Maj. (since Lt.-Col.)	Sandford, D. A., D.S.O.	16/12/15	4 /9/18	United Service Club, Pall Mall, London.	Posted to command 355 S.B.
Maj.	Lowe, C. E. B., D.S.O., M.C.	8/ 9/18	June, 1919	Constitutional Club, London, W.	Demobilised with Cadre.
Capt. (since Maj.)	Bennett, A. C.	7/ 1/16	19/ 8/16	Stanton Vicarage, West Hartlepool, Durham.	To U.K. to command 186 S.B.
Capt.	Platnauer, M.	7/ 1/16	3/ 4/17	St. Olaf, West Cliff, Bournemouth.	Appointed Adjt. 45th H.A. Group.
„	Lush, M. S., M.C.	18/12/15	10 /5/18	24, High Croft Terrace, Brighton.	Appointed Staff Capt. III. Corps, Counter Batteries.
„	Somerville, R. A. E., M.C., M.M.	22/ 9/16	13/ 5/19	c/o Messrs. Cox & Co., 16, Charing Cross, London, S.W.	Posted 420 S.B, Army of Rhine.
„	Grant, F., M.C.	8/ 1/17	13/ 8/17	St.Michael's Mount, Shire Oak Rd., Headingley, Leeds.	Invalided to U.K. (shell wound). Subsequently invalided out of service

Rank	Name			Address	Remarks
Capt.	Opie, W. L.	8/ 6/18	5/ 8/18	9, Leinster Mansions, Langland Gardens, Finchley Rd., London, N.W. 3.	Evacuated sick.
Lieut.	Clark, G.	7/ 1/16	14/ 9/16	The Green, Seaton Carew, Durham.	Invalided to U. K. (wounded).
"	Lovegrove, C. G.	29/ 6/16	11/ 4/18	76, Bolingbroke Grove, Wandsworth Common, S.W.	Invalided to U. K. (bomb wound).
"	Hopkins, E. S.	13/ 7/17	3/ 2/19	Brookside, Moss Lane, Pinner.	To U.K. for demobilisation.
"	Hoggan, R.	3/ 9/17	14/ 4/19	Comely Bank, College Rd., Dulwich, S.E.	"
"	Chamberlain, G. C. L.	15/ 1/18	14 /4/19	Lynton, Priory Road, St. Denys, Southampton.	"
"	Watts, C.	12/ 7/18	3/12/18	14, Hazlewood Terrace, Peverell, Plymouth.	Retained for Home duty whilst on leave.
"	Platt, S.	21/10/18	14/ 4/19	343, Wigan Road, Deane, Bolton, Lancs.	To U.K. for demobilisation.
2nd Lt. (since (Lt.)	Cassidy, D. M., M.C.	18/12/15	28/ 2/17	St. James' Vicarage, Westgate-on-Sea.	Appointed Orderly Officer, IV. Corps, Counter Batteries, thence to R.A.F.
2nd Lt.	*de Beer, B. H.	20/ 9/16	10/ 7/17	75, London Rd., Dunedin, New Zealand.	Killed in action.
"	Mason, L. S.	13/ 7/17	18/ 5/18	Wayside, Wilton Road, Shirley, Southampton.	Posted to Fourth Army A.A.D.C.

* Killed in Action.

Rank.	Name.	Period with Unit.		Home Address.	Remarks.
		From	To		
2nd Lt.	Gardiner, J.	26/9/17	4/9/18	The Hollies, Cameron Park, Edinburgh.	Posted to 5th Fld. Surv. Bn., R.E.
"	Clarke, W. R.	19/10/17	24/9/18	61, Addingbourne Road, Shepherd's Bush, London.	Posted to III. Corps H.A.
"	Storer, C.	22/4/18	31/10/18	13, Bruce Grove, Watford, Herts.	Invalided to U.K. (Influenza).
"	Selous-Jones, C. R.	10/5/18	14/6/18	Bohanam House, Gloucester.	Invalided to U.K. (gassed).
"	Betts, G. K.	29/5/18	Aug., 1919	13, Grange Road, Woodthorpe, Nottingham.	Demobilised with Equipment Guard.
"	Hill, R.	29/5/18	20/9/18	Lizard Point, Cornwall.	Invalided to U.K. (sick).
"	McComber, J. L.	23/10/18	9/2/19	186, Court Street North, Port Arthur, Ontario, Canada.	Repatriated (Canada).

PART IV

NOMINAL ROLL OF N.C.O.'s AND MEN WHO, HAVING JOINED THE BATTERY DURING ITS FORMATION IN ENGLAND, SERVED WITH IT THROUGHOUT ITS FIGHTING IN FRANCE.†

REGTL. NO.	RANK.	NAME.	ADDRESS.	DATE OF CASUALTY.	NATURE OF CASUALTY.
337852	B.Q.M.S.	Gilmour, J. H., M.M.	1, Steven Street, West Hartlepool.	9/ 2/19	Demobilised.
337988	Sgt.	Bate, W.	22, Richmond Street, West Hartlepool.	24/ 6/19	Demobilised with Cadre.
337734	„	Birks, A. H., D.C.M.	2, Wharton Street, West Hartlepool.	27/ 1/19	Demobilised.
338061	„	Brignall, J. T., M.S.M.	2A, Benson Street, Linthorpe, Middlesborough.	18/12/19	„
149338	„	Carter, E.	12, Brunswick Street, Hartlepool.	19/ 2/17 8/11/17 8/ 2/19	To U.K. (wounded) Reposted. Demobilised.
338059	„	Harrison, F., M.M.	30, Bush Street, Middlesborough.	29/12/19	Demobilised.
28944	„	Hopkins, F. G.	32, Church Street, Maidstone.	24/ 6/19	Demobilised with Cadre.
59741	„	Trueman, R.	27, Bowden Street, Macclesfield.	Aug., 1919	Demobilised with Equipment Guard.

† A few of these spent short periods in hospital, but were subsequently reposted to the Battery.

REGTL. No.	RANK.	NAME.	ADDRESS.	DATE OF CASUALTY.	NATURE OF CASUALTY.
338069	Cpl.	Dennett, W. H. G.	47, Fernville Terrace, Murray St., W. Hartlepool.	24 /6/19	Demobilised with Cadre.
337627	,,	Graham, T. J.	Middlesboro' Hotel, Hartlepool.	13/12/18	Demobilised.
67269	,,	Smith, R.	23, Commercial Road, Spalding, Lincs.	4/ 1/19	,,
59242	,,	Webb, A. T.	29, Baker Street, Northampton.	24/ 6/19	Demobilised with Cadre.
338005	Bdr.	Ashett, E.	11, Church Street, Chilton Lane, Ferryhill, Durham	23/12/19	Demobilised.
66065	,,	Armitage, T., M.M.	61, Rose Street, Huxley Road, York.	21/ 1/19	,,
365645	Sig./Bdr.	Dakers, W. M.	Milton of Craigie, Dundee, N.B.	24/ 6/19	Demobilised with Cadre.
66005	Bdr.	Fitzpatrick, W.	Tudhoe Village, Spennymoor, Durham.	Aug., 1919	Demobilised with Equipment Guard.
338068	,,	Rusby, H. R., M.M.	9, Victor Street, York.	9/ 2/19	Demobilised.
338066	L./Bdr.	Hooper, D.	13, Spring Street, Rise Carri, Darlington.	22/12/19	Demobilised.
66029	,,	Kavanagh, W.	Kyliomore, The Rover, co. Kilkenny.	3/ 4/19	Posted to Army of Occupation (volunteer).

	L./Bdr.				
67388	L./Bdr.	Pett, E. F.	26, Kitchener Road, East Finchley.	24/ 6/19	Demobilised with Cadre.
68264	"	Rose, F. R., M.M.	White Horse Road, East Bergholt, Suffolk.	18/11/18	To Hospital while on leave in U.K.
338060	Gnr.	Allison, A	6, Gable Terrace, Wheatley Hill, Durham.	18/12/19	Demobilised.
59264	"	Braybrook, G. W.	2, Lawson Street, Kettering, Northants.	24/ 6/19	Demobilised with Cadre.
59656	Sig.	Butlin, G.	Drayton Place, Daventry, Northants.	24/ 6/19	" " "
67049	"	Dakin, T.	Columbia Villa, Burlingham Road, Eltringham, Cheshire.	2/ 4/19	To Hospital.
58907	"	Edwards, W. H.	New Inn, Council Schools, Pen-Coder, S. Wales.	29/ 1/19	Demobilised.
338062	Gnr.	Evans, G. F.	12, Haymore Street, Middlesbrough.	18/12/19	"
68695	"	Fallick, W. S.	Aldingbourne, Chichester, Sussex.	13/ 5/19	Posted to Army of Occupation.
59666	"	Houghton, G. T.	8, Lutterworth Road, Daventree, Northants.	24/ 6/19	Demobilised with Cadre.
58936	Sig.	Houldsworth, A.	30, Regents Place, near Keighley, Yorks.	24/ 6/19	" " "
365609	"	Moyes, R. C.	Synburn, Broughty Ferry, N.B.	24/ 6/19	" " "
67176	"	Rensch, E. A.	23, Wilton Square, Islington.	20/ 1/19	To Hospital.

Regtl. No.	Rank.	Name.	Address.	Date of Casualty.	Nature of Casualty.
337633	Gnr.	Stainthorpe, T.	46, Plevna Street, West Hartlepool.	2/ 2/19	Demobilised.
67286	,,	Thole, W.	7, Vine Cottage, Factory Road, Uxbridge Road, Hanwell.	24/ 6/19	Demobilised with Cadre.
68724	,,	Vickery, E.	50, Heaton Road, Peckham, London.	7/ 6/19	Posted to Army of Occupation.
68473	,,	Waller, E. J.	10, Ada Terrace, Southwick, Sussex.	13/ 5/19	Posted to Army of Occupation.
59252	,,	Wykes, A. D.	66, St. Vincent Road, Dartford.	16/ 2/19	Demobilised.

PART V.

REMAINDER OF ORIGINAL UNIT ON ARRIVAL IN FRANCE, MAY 30TH, 1916.

REGTL. No.	RANK.	NAME.	ADDRESS.	DATE OF CASUALTY.	NATURE OF CASUALTY.
16121	B.S.M.	Cook, M. F.	12, Arlesford Road, Stockwell, London.	11/10/16	To Hospital.
7196	B.Q.M.S.	Murray, F. W.	51, Commercial Street, Leith.	5/ 2/17	To Home Establishment.
6138	Smith, Sgt.	Martin, W. H.	11, Harworth Street, Bolton, Lancs.	18/ 5/18	To U.K. (time expired).
11762	Sgt.	Arbon, G.	12E, Peabody Estate, Vauxhall Road, London.	20/12/16	Posted to 13 S.B.
20059	,,	*Collyer, J., M.M.	—	24/11/17	Killed in action.
29269	,,	Clarke, L. L.	29, Rednall Terrace, Hammersmith, London.	14/ 9/17	Posted to 135 S.B.
58257	,,	*Duckels, C. F.	10, Sunny Bank Avenue, Horsforth, Leeds.	20/ 7/17	Killed in action.
67424	,,	Hedges, F. T.	3, Holmfield Cottages, East End Road, E. Finchley, London.	12/12/17	Invalided to U.K.
21255	,,	Nethercott, A.	85, Lewes Road, Newhaven, Sussex.	9/ 4/17	Posted to 242 S.B.
58924	,,	Toop, A. V., M.M.	27, Seventh Avenue, Bush Hill Park, London.	31/ 8/17	To Cadet School, U.K.

* Killed in action or died of wounds or from other causes.

REGTL. NO.	RANK.	NAME.	ADDRESS.	DATE OF CASUALTY.	NATURE OF CASUALTY.
337645	Sgt.	*Ward, C. M.	6, Balmoral Terrace, York	15/ 3/17	To U.K. (Munitions).
5265	,,	Winter, R.	20, St. Oswald's Terrace, West Hartlepool.	5/ 1/17	Posted to 87 S.B.
53617	Smith/Sgt.	Turnbull, M. A.	21, Colne Street, Middlesbrough.	15/ 5/17	To Hospital.
338056	Cpl.	Brice, W. S., M.S.M.	162, Westgate, Guisboro', Yorks.	30/ 9/18	To Cadet School, U.K.
337773	,,	Coussons, J.	Greenside, Greatham, Durham.	1/10/18	Invalided to U.K.
30830	,,	Crouch, R. W.	Prior Wood Cottage, Hertford Heath, Herts.	20/10/16	,, ,,
6089	,,	Griveson, M. N.	22, Baltic Street, Hartlepool.	27/ 4/17	,, ,,
5700	,,	Jenkins, D.	3, Robinson Street, West Hartlepool.	14/10/16	,, ,,
6143	,,	Lodge, R. C.	Etherley, Bishop Auckland, co. Durham.	5/ 2/18	To Cadet School.
66051	,,	Randall, J.	4, Short Street, Upper Edmonton, London.	28/ 3/17	Invalided to U.K. (accidental injury).
52258	,,	Slaymaker, A. W.	51, London Road, Wembley, London.	4/ 1/17	Invalided to U.K.
50193	,,	Wright, A. E.	Wistow, Huntington.	25/ 2/17	To Home Establishment
62376	Bdr.	Bean, H.	Bagdon Hall, Denby Dale, Huddersfield.	6/10/17	To Cadet School, U.K.

	No.	Name	Address	Date	Remarks
Bdr.	5646	Cole, W.	47, Synge Street, Dublin.	16/12/16	Invalided to U.K.
,,	45600	Cunningham, A., M.M.	Woodville, Ontario, Canada.	9/10/16	,,
,,	67334	Hills, F. W.	20, Golden Lane, London, E.C.	4/12/17	Posted XV. Corps H.A.
,,	56704	*McMullen, F. J.	9, Grove Avenue, Hemsworth, near Wakefield.	27/ 8/16	Killed in action.
,,	6058	Peart, I. G.	5, William Street, Chilton Lane, Ferryhill, Durham.	14/ 7/17	Invalided to U.K.
,,	337675	Porritt, J.	40, Robinson Street, West Hartlepool.	1/ 4/18	To Hospital.
,,	337776	Thomas, A. E.	7, South Crescent, Hartlepool.	29/ 8/18	Invalided to U.K
,,	59746	Yeomans, B.	8, Bouverie Street, Northampton.	17/ 9/16	,,
Sig./Bdr.	68293	Robinson, W.	Brayfield, Northants.	28/ 9/16	To Hospital.
A./Bdr.	6140	Brown, T.	Popular House, 11, Roseberry Terrace, Shildon, Durham.	26/ 2/17	Posted to Transportation Depot, R.E.
,,	5882	Mitchell, T. D.	52, Lowthian Road, West Hartlepool.	14/ 9/16	Invalided to U.K.
,,	5869	Oliver, H.	33, Melrose Street, West Hartlepool.	4/ 9/16	,,
L./Bdr.	337694	Armstrong, T.	18, Bedford Street, East Hartlepool.	15/ 9/16 July 17– Aug. 18	,, Reposted ; then to Hospital.
,,	59357	Bennett, F.	26, Gasholder Terrace, Hunslet, Leeds.	21/ 9/18	Invalided to U.K.

* Killed in action or died of wounds or from other causes.

Regtl. No.	Rank.	Name.	Address.	Date of Casualty.	Nature of Casualty.
66940	Gnr.	Aaron, B.	207, Beeston Hill, Leeds.	24/ 3/17	Invalided to U.K.
5729	,,	Andrews, A.	43, Frederick Street, Hartlepool.	16/ 9/16	,,
337593	,,	Armstrong, R.	3, Pelham Street, Hartlepool.	28/ 5/18	,,
5630	,,	Arnison, W.	31, Burbank Street, West Hartlepool.	7/ 8/17	,,
5788	,,	*Barr, J. W.	13, Carr Street, West Hartlepool.	4/ 9/16	Died of wounds.
65903	,,	Barnett, C. S.	31, Leighton Street, East Croydon, Surrey.	27/ 2/17	Posted to Transportation Depot, R.E.
65900	,,	Barnett, W. H.	20, Leighton Street, East Croydon, Surrey.	27/ 2/17	
337582	,,	Bartholomew, A.	42, Rockeby Street, Hartlepool.	29/ 4/18	Invalided to U.K.
62375	,,	Bean, F.	Bagdon Hall, Denby Dale, Huddersfield.	4/12/16	To IV. Corps H.A.
58831	Sig.	Besant, R.	Seale Hayne, Newton Abbot, S. Devon.	11/11/16, 13/12/18–7/ 2/19	To U.K. (under age). Reposted and demobilised.
5511	Gnr.	Black, H.	43, Grey Street, West Hartlepool.	10/ 9/16	Invalided to U.K.
5658	Sig.	Blackburn, W.	49, Colenso Street, West Hartlepool.	24/10/16	,,

337871	Gnr.	Boagey, H.	3, Croft Street, West Hartlepool.	22/7/17	Invalided to U.K.
6069	,,	Boast, R. D.	1, Ross Terrace, Ferryhill.	16/9/16	,, ,, ,,
66933	,,	Boothroyd, H.	17, Fieldhouse Road, Huddersfield.	25/7/17	,, ,, ,,
59703	,,	Boswell, H. L.	83, Milton Street, Northampton.	30/6/16	,, ,, ,,
338005	,,	Brice, E.	49, Church Street, Guisborough, York.	1/7/17	,, ,, ,,
49883	,,	Cain, T.	28, West Street, Leadgate, Durham.	27/9/16	,, ,, ,,
66998	,,	Catt, S.	West Cross, Rolvenden, Kent.	5/4/18	To Hospital.
64172	,,	*Collick, J. H., M.M.	Henry Street, Reading, Berks.	8/11/16	Invalided to U.K. (subsequently died).
2390	,,	Collick, T.	1, Buckwood Street, Burley, Leeds.	3/12/16	Invalided to U.K.
58561	,,	Collins, J.	4, Gaines Street, Marine Town, Sheerness.	24/12/16	,, ,,
337803	,,	Davison, G.	63, Mary Street, Hartlepool.	28/9/16	To Hospital (gassed).
5967	,,	Dawson, W. H.	Dene Holm Terrace, Horden.	12/9/16	Invalided to U.K.
59368	,,	*Day, A. V.	31, Hampton Street, Hessland, Chesterfield, Derbyshire.	10/7/17	Killed in action.

* Killed in action or died of wounds or from other causes.

Regtl. No.	Rank.	Name.	Address.	Date of Casualty.	Nature of Casualty.
5877	Gnr.	Doyle, F.	8, St. Mary Street, West Hartlepool.	27/ 2/17	Invalided to U.K.
66876	,,	Duckels, A. H.	64, Mistress Lane, Armley, Leeds.	21/10/17	,, ,,
5580	,,	Dunn, J.	26, Hill Street, Long Hill, West Hartlepool.	25/ 2/18	,, ,,
58905	,,	*Edser, G. H.	White House, Peaslake, Guildford, Surrey.	19/11/17	Died of wounds.
59171	,,	*Edwards, J. S.	299, Allison Street, Govanhill, Glasgow.	12/ 8/17	Killed in action.
67093	,,	Elliott, W. J.	St. John's Chapel, co. Durham.	7/ 9/16	To Hospital.
6072	,,	*Eltringham, T.	16, Feversham Terrace, Ferryhill.	27/ 8/16	Killed in action.
5455	,,	Forder, F. W.	36, Crimdén Street, West Hartlepool.	17/ 7/16	To Hospital.
67185	,,	Frankland, H.	10, Ross Terrace, Bramley, Leeds.	13/ 9/16	Invalided to U.K.
39038	,,	Fleming, P.	5, Lower Grand Cause, Dublin.	4/ 7/16	,, ,,
5796	,,	*Flewker, H.	3, Sheriffs Street, West Hartlepool.	11/ 7/16	Died from injuries received in railway accident.

No.	Name	Rank	Address	Date	Remarks
5607	Gardner, J. T.	Gnr.	21, Wards Terrace, Hartlepool.	26/ 7/17	Invalided to U.K.
5586	Gill, W. T.	"	134, Alma Street, West Hartlepool.	14/ 8/16	" "
6097	Herron, G. A.	"	22, Front Street, Shotton Colliery, Durham.	19/12/16	To Hospital
59377	Hill, W. J.	"	24, Boundary Road, St. Albans, Herts.	April, 1917	" "
5830	Hodgman, C. E.	"	14, Bramley Street, West Hartlepool.	12/ 1/17	" "
5833	Hodgson, S.	"	41, Bedford Street, West Hartlepool.	16/ 8/17	To U.K. (released for Munition work).
67991	Hook, H. T.	"	"The Quarter," Tenderton, Kent.	14/10/16	Invalided to U.K.
5816	Jenkinson, H.	"	12, Coverdale Street, Hartlepool.	8/ 7/16	To U.K. (released for Munition work).
337681	*Jenson, H. W.	"	25, Essex Street, West Hartlepool.	24/11/17	Killed in action.
5924	Ling-Bean, D.	"	9, Pit Street, Trimdon Colliery, Durham.	30/ 3/17	To Hospital.
5696	Lott, G.	"	36, Burbank Street, West Hartlepool.	26/ 2/17	Posted to Transportation Depot, R.E.
337859	*Mayes, E.	W./Gnr.	15, Wath St., Hartlepool.	16/ 9/17	Killed in action.
4256	McCarthy, P.	Gnr.	Scarte, Douglas, co. Cork, Ireland.	Mar., 1917	Invalided to U.K.
337710	McTernan, C.	"	Stainton Street, West Hartlepool.	21/ 9/18	" "

* Killed in action or died of wounds or from other causes.

REGTL. NO.	RANK.	NAME.	ADDRESS.	DATE OF CASUALTY.	NATURE OF CASUALTY.
337809	Gnr.	Moore, R. W.	75, Great Frederick Street, Hartlepool.	22/ 9/18	Invalided to U.K.
62192	,,	Morgan, A.	8, Heathfield Terrace, Swanley, Kent.	18/ 9/16	,, ,,
70518	,,	Nixon, W.	896, Romford Road, Manor Park, Essex.	14/12/16	,, ,,
66904	,,	Parkin, A.	54, Forster Street, Sunderland.	24/ 6/19	To 91 S.B.
5887	,,	Peppert, R.	15, Derby Street, West Hartlepool.	8/12/16	Invalided to U.K.
68665	,,	Riley, P.	21, Mary Street, St. George's East, London.	23/ 6/17	,, ,,
68637	,,	Robertson, W.	94, Are Street, Barking, Essex.	20/10/18	To Hospital (accidental injury).
66980	,,	Steel, D. A.	45, Wyndham Road, Kingston, London.	15/ 3/17	To Hospital.
68340	,,	Schulte, A.	13, Bowness Road, Catford, London.	4/ 6/17	To Hospital (gassed).
5524	,,	Seago, W. C.	53, Clarendon Road, West Hartlepool.	19/ 6/17	Invalided to U.K.
67081	,,	Shaw, S. T.	5, Chester Street, Barrow-in-Furness.	13/ 3/17	Posted to Transportation Depot, R.E.
67283	,,	*Smith, W. H.	24, Western Road, Ealing, London.	12/ 5/17	Killed in action.

	Gnr.	Streeting, A.	44, Longmore Street, West Hartlepool.	16/ 9/16	Invalided to U.K.
5549	,,	*Thompson, A. M.	Clapper's Farm, Glazeley, near Reading, Berks.	24/ 8/16	Died of wounds.
69713	,,	Waller, J. T.	4, Norfolk Terrace, East-field Road, S. Lincs.	26/ 3/18	Invalided to U.K.
67002	,,	Walker, J.	26, Burn Valley Road, West Hartlepool.	10/ 7/17	To Hospital.
6032	,,	Ware, O.	23, Hyde Place, Llanhilleth, Monmouth.	5/ 8/17	Invalided to U.K.
59608	,,	Warren, W. G.	Chapel Row, Therfield, near Royston, Herts.	12/ 2/17	Posted to IV. Corps H.A.
68687	,,	Watson, A. S	5, Rillington Place, St. Mark's Rd., Nottingham.	15/ 9/16	Invalided to U.K.
3188	,,	Webb, S.	127, Chapter Road, Willesden Green.	16/ 9/16	,,
66060	,,	Wheeler, C. E.	25, Meadvale Road, Woodside, Croydon.	16/ 7/17	,,
64263	,,	Whitlock, W.	High Street, Silverston, Northants.	28/ 9/18	,,
59744	,,	Wills, W.	11, Evesby Road, Hampstead, London.	9/ 4/18	,,
64097	,,	Wilkinson, J.	83, Parkside Road, Bradford, Yorks.	15/ 7/17	,,
6074	,,	Wilson, R.	26, Ashbourne Grove, Halifax, Yorks.	15/10/16	,,
67201	,,	Wright, W. E.	26, Kent St., Middlesbrough.	19/10/16	,,
6038					

* Killed in action or died of wounds or from other causes.

PART VI.

Reinforcements.†

Regtl. No.	Rank.	Name.	Address.	Period of Service.	Nature of Casualty.
358202	B.S.M.	Finch, F. C., D.C.M.	79, Springfield Road, Northfleet, Kent.	16/ 2/17—24/ 6/19	Demobilised with Cadre.
34588	,,	Marshall, G.	(Father) Limbrick, Goring, Sussex.	8/12/16—26/ 6/17	Posted to 261 S.B. (since died).
13535	B.Q.M.S.	Collinson, R.	25, Lenord Street, Stockton-on-Tees.	24/11/17—19/ 3/18	Posted to 106 S.B.
13992	,,	Gilpin, W.	12, Carberry Terrace, Burley Lodge Road, Leeds.	15/ 8/17—19/11/17	Posted to 19th H.A. group.
326508	Sgt.	*Aird, J.	87, Radnor Street, Clydebank, Scotland.	15/ 1/18— 5/ 3/19	Volunteer, Army of Occupation. Posted to 2nd Army.
13660	,,	*Jackson, W.	8, Brunton Street, West Hartlepool.	15/ 1/18— 6/ 2/19	Demobilised.
18274	Cpl.	*Bolton, T. W.	8, Bridge Street, Londonderry, Ireland.	15/ 1/18—26/ 1/18	To Hospital.
39529	,,	*Boreham, L.	49, Vineyard Street, Colchester, Essex.	15/ 1/18—18/ 1/19	To U.K. to complete colour service.

296213	Cpl.	Bottrill, J. N.	89, Victoria Park Road, South Hackney, E. 9.	15/ 8/17—24/ 6/19	Demobilised with Cadre.
50896	,,	Clarke, C. A.	24, Caroline Street, Hetton-le-Hole, Durham.	22/ 4/18—10/ 2/19	Demobilised.
102795	,,	Davies, W. H.	Bryn Celyn, Penrhidyn, Clydach, Swansea.	23/10/16—20/ 1/19	,,
48999	,,	Dodd, J., M.M.	21, Plex Street, Tunstall, Staffs.	24/ 7/16— 3/ 2/19	,,
34480	,,	*Golding, H. J.	High Street, Kidlington, Oxford.	15/ 1/18—24/ 6/19	Demobilised with Cadre.
13011	,,	*Hanlon, P., M.M.	36, Back Brook Street, Monk Wearmouth, Sunderland.	15/ 1/18—29/12/18	Demobilised.
15828	,,	Lee, H.	20, Elmsfield Street, Cheetham Hill, Manchester.	6/ 8/17—27/ 5/19	Posted to Army of Occupation.
14???	,,	Small, C. J.	Rugby House, Oxford Street, Clacton-on-Sea.	13/ 8/17— 6/ 3/19	To Hospital.
59787	,,	Winn, T. W.	10, Medina Road, Holloway, London, N.	18/ 7/16— 7/ 2/19	Demobilised.
72074	Bdr.	Burn, E. F.	Loyalty House, Church Gate, Stockport, Cheshire.	19/10/16—12/ 8/17	To Hospital.
139470	,,	Double, H.	36, Knowsley Road, Battersea, London.	23/ 6/17—15/ 4/19	Posted to Army of Occupation.

* From 190 Siege Battery (January, 1918).

† Many of the men mentioned in this roll, though posted as reinforcements to the Battery, had already seen service in France with other batteries.

REGTL No.	RANK.	NAME.	ADDRESS.	PERIOD OF SERVICE.	NATURE OF CASUALTY.
136618	Bdr.	*Driffield, W.	33, Cameron Road, West Hartlepool.	15/ 1/18— 7/ 9/18	Invalided to U.K.
78317	,,	Edwards, W. S., M.M.	105, Peter Hill Road, Springburn, Glasgow.	20/ 8/16— 7/ 4/18	,, ,,
89576	,,	*Henchcliffe, G.	117A, Branstone Road, Burton-on-Trent.	15/ 1/18—14 4/19	Posted to Army of Occupation.
9517	,,	Mason, J.	3, Victoria Row, Kempsey, near Worcester.	24/ 9/16—18/ 7/17	Invalided to U.K.
21431	,,	†Mason, J.	Alexandra Villas, Great Wakering, Essex.	21/ 1/17—13/ 7/17	Died of wounds.
285085	,,	Munt, J. W.	101, Craven Park Road, S. Tottenham, London.	23/ 6/17— 3/ 1/19	Demobilised.
36947	,,	O'Keefe, C.	Lacken Roe, Glanmire, co. Cork, Ireland.	15/ 1/18—20/ 6/19	To U.K. to complete colour service.
40033	,,	Ott, W.	Gownboys, Charterhouse, Godalming, Surrey.	April '18—15/ 1/19	To U.K. to complete colour service.
478923	,,	*Tillin, A. A.	9, Nether Street, Alton, Hants.	15/ 1/18—20/ 1/19	Demobilised.
120718	,,	Wyse, J.	6, Prince Albert Terrace, Helensburgh, Scotland.	20/11/17—25/12/18	,,

No.	Rank	Name	Address	Dates	Disposition
34710	L./Bdr.	Butt, P.	Bailiffs Course, St. Andrews, Guernsey.	13/10/18—19/ 5/19	Repatriated to Channel Islands.
94567	,,	Clarke, H.	43, Thornaby Road, Thornaby-on-Tees, Yorks.	22/ 4/18—14/ 4/19	Posted to Army of Occupation.
19512	,,	Costello, J.	122, Townsend Street, Dublin.	6/ 7/18—28/ 9/18	Invalided to U.K.
65710	,,	Davies, H. A	127, Scotland Grew Road, Ponder's End, London, N.	20/ 3/17—20/ 1/19	Demobilised.
172320	,,	Dixon, H. W.	6, St. Stephens Crescent, Bayswater.	22/ 4/18— 5/ 8/18	To Hospital.
88389	,,	*Hawkins, J. W.	7, Salisbury Road, West Ealing, London.	15/ 1/18—15/ 4/19	Posted to Army of Occupation.
89588	,,	*Hudson, J.	188, Belvedere Road, Burton-on-Trent.	15/ 1/18—28/ 9/18	Invalided to U.K.
80220	,,	*Jones, I.	Symlog House, Slomsymlog, Bow, South Wales.	15/ 1/18—26/12/18	Demobilised.
306519	Sig./L./Bdr.	Pritchard, J	59, Scott Street, Perth, Scotland.	28/ 7/17—13/ 1/19	,,
76482	L./Bdr.	Moss, A. W.	Old Buckingham, near Attleborough, Norfolk.	17/ 9/16—27/ 1/19	,,
116754	Gnr.	Alford, W.	Lower Coombe, Cadeleigh, near Tiverton, Devon.	20/10/18—13/ 5/19	Posted to Army of Occupation.
155668	,,	*Almond, R.	Cronton Farm, Cronton, near Prescott, Lancs.	15/ 1/18—28/ 9/18	Invalided to U.K.

* From 190 Siege Battery (Jan. 1918). ‡ Killed in action, or died of wounds or from other causes.

Regtl. No.	Rank.	Name.	Address.	Period of Service.	Nature of Casualty.
128063	Gnr.	Anderson, T. G.	81, Spencer Street, Heaton, Newcastle-on-Tyne	22/ 4/18—28/ 9/18	Invalided to U.K.
150793	Sig.	Anderson, W. H.	12–14, Denison Street, Liverpool.	15/ 8/17— 2/ 1/19	Demobilised whilst on leave.
155659	Gnr.	*Angus, J.	43, Clarendon Terrace, Skerton, Lancs.	15/ 1/18— 3/ 4/19	Posted to Army of Occupation.
196813	,,	*Ankritt, H.	Yockleton, near Shrewsbury, Shropshire.	22/ 4/18—28/ 1/19	Demobilised.
176454	,,	Armitage, H.	70, Woodsley Road, Leeds	21/ 2/18—23/ 4/18	To Hospital.
334439	,,	Arnold, A. H.	7, Queen Street, Poole, Dorset.	13/ 8/17—24/ 6/19	Demobilised with Cadre.
186051	,,	Atherley, A.	69, Robert Street, Newton Heath, Manchester.	21/ 4/18—14/ 4/19	Posted to Army of Occupation.
89727	,,	*Atkinson, H.	102, Station Parade, Harrogate, Yorks.	15/ 1/18—28/ 9/18	Invalided to U.K.
188426	Sig.	Atkinson, T.	24, Castlegate, Malton, Yorks.	23/ 4/18— 5/ 3/19	Posted to Army of Occupation.
179095	Gnr.	Austin, E. J.	1, Bockhanger Cottages, Kennington, near Ashford, Kent.	22/ 4/18—Aug. '19	Demobilised with Equipment Guard.
178145	,,	*Aylett, H.	7, Whiting Square, Ospringe, near Faversham, Kent.	15/ 1/18— 3/ 4/19	Posted to Army of Occupation.

No.	Rank	Name	Address	Dates	Remarks
63393	Gnr.	Baillie, W.	114, Stewart Street, Carluke, Lanark, Scotland.	30/ 9/18—24/ 6/19	Demobilised with Cadre.
38908	,,	Baker, L.	Beach Croft, Stourbridge.	30/ 9/18— 8/ 2/19	Demobilised.
124668	,,	Baldwin, J. E.	32, Nantymelyn Terrace. Coed-Ely, Tonyrefail, Glamorgan.	30/ 9/18—28/ 4/19	Posted to Army of Occupation.
280079	,,	Baldry, R.	Saxlingham, near Norwich.	22/ 4/16—24/ 6/19	Demobilised with Cadre.
204052	,,	Ball, A. R.	Parliament Street,Stroud, Gloucester.	30/ 9/18— 5/ 3/19	Posted to Army of Occupation.
101277	,,	‡Balls, O. H.	Turnpike Farm, Carleton Road, Attleborough, folk.	17/12/16—14/ 6/17	Killed in action.
141518	Sig.	Bancroft, G. W.	4, Grovedale Road, Mossley Hill, Liverpool.	15/ 8/17—13 /5/19	Posted to Army of Occupation.
98609	Gnr.	*‡Banfield, H.	Carn Greg, St. Austell, Cornwall.	15/ 1/18—27/ 5/18	Killed in action.
196620	,,	Banger, H. S.	"Sportsman" Inn, Pegwell Bay, Kent.	22/ 4/18— 9/ 2/19	Demobilised.
113757	,,	*Barker, H.	11, South View, Frizinghall, Bradford.	15/ 1/18—14/ 4/19	Posted to Army of Occupation.
169253	,,	Barnes, A. G.	27, Fuller Street, Kettering, Northants.	22/ 4/18—15/ 1/19	Demobilised.
117400	,,	Barnett, H.	29, Newborough Street, Bootham, Yorks.	13/ 7/17—15/ 4/19	Posted to Army of Occupation.

* From 190 Siege Battery (Jan. 1918).   ‡ Killed in action, or died of wounds or from other causes.

REGTL. NO.	RANK.	NAME.	ADDRESS.	PERIOD OF SERVICE.	NATURE OF CASUALTY.
91231	Gnr.	Barrett, A. J.	25, Victoria Road, Bedminster, Bristol.	22/ 4/16—28/ 9/18	Invalided to U.K.
80747	,,	Barwick, J. T.	28, West Lane, Haworth, Yorkshire.	17/12/16—26/12/18	Demobilised.
110078	,,	Bateman, J.	Abbott Ann, Andover.	22/ 4/18—Aug. '19.	Demobilised with Equipment Guard.
123140	,,	Beeston, C.	Little Sugnall, Eccleshall, Staffs.	13/ 7/17— 6/ 2/19	Demobilised.
113818	,,	*Bell, G.	North End, Swineshead, near Boston, Lincs.	15/ 1/18—28/ 4/19	Posted to Army of Occupation.
92922	,,	*Bell, F. R.	Garrigill, Alston, Cumberland.	15/ 1/18— 3/ 4/19	Posted to Army of Occupation.
157331	,,	Bennett, W.	31, Park Road, Plumstead, Kent.	13/ 8/17—25/12/17	Invalided to U.K.
78123	,,	Bicknell, C. H.	108, Putney Road, Handsworth, Birmingham.	8/ 9/18—10/ 1/19	Demobilised.
40695	,,	*Bishop, E.	10, Keyford Terrace, Somerset.	15/ 1/18— 9/ 4/18	To Hospital.
146322	Sig.	Blackburn, J.	56, Grey Street, Burnley.	25/ 4/17—25/ 2/19	,,
178972	,,	Bodley, H.	39, Darlington Road, West Norwood, London.	22/ 4/18—14/ 7/18	,,

No.	Rank	Name	Address	Date	Remarks
104231	Gnr.	Bollom, R.	Kenton Lodge, Gosforth, Newcastle-on-Tyne.	1/ 1/17—15/11/18	„
150101	Sig.	Booth, J. J.	7, Dudley Road, Pendlebury, Lancs.	15/ 8/17—Mar. '19	„
160082	Gnr.	Bowden, J.	234, Guinness Buildings, Pages Walk, Bermondsey.	20/10/18—14/ 4/19	Posted to Army of Occupation.
194287	„	Booty, F.	66, Freehold Road, Ipswich.	23/ 4/18—23/ 5/18	To Hospital.
70775	„	Botcher, J.	14, Boleyn Road, East Ham, London.	30/ 5/17—26/ 7/17	Invalided to U.K.
98502	„	Bosier, F. G.	17A, East Street, Southampton, Hants.	28/ 2/18—14/ 4/19	Posted to Army of Occupation.
67802		Boxall, E. C.	20, Alexander Road, Addlestone, Surrey.	7/12/16—27/ 2/17	Invalided to U.K.
153318	„	Boyes, W. E.	128, Pawsons Road, West Croydon, Surrey.	22/ 4/18— 8/ 2/19	Demobilised.
150106	Sig.	‡Bradbury,	17, Kendal Road, Poulton, Seacombe, Cheshire	15/ 8/17— 7/11/18	Died from influenza.
89723	Gr.	*Brigham, R.	Rainton, Yorkshire.	15/ 1/18— 2/ 2/19	Demobilised.
104903	„	Brett, T. D.	2, Park Place, East Finchley, N. 2.	13/ 8/17— 3/ 4/19	Posted to Army of Occupation.
86534	„	Brewer, H. W. C. G.	6, Waldeck Road, Chiswick, London.	6/ 7/17—24/ 6/19	Demobilised with Cadre.

* From 190 Siege Battery (Jan. 1918).   ‡ Killed in action, or died of wounds or from other causes.

Regtl. No.	Rank.	Name.	Address.	Period of Service.	Nature of Casualty.
179767	Gnr	Broadbent, A.	21, Forest Street, Oldham, Lancs.	20/10/18—29/10/18	To Hospital.
72877	,,	Brown, G.	Comberford, Tamworth, Staffs.	30/ 7/16—27/ 1/18	,, ,,
136605	,,	*Brownless, E.	1, Usher Road, Ludworth, Durham.	15/ 1/18—24/10/18	,, ,,
68445	,,	Brown, S.	Town Head, Ballymoney, Leitrim.	2/ 7/16—14/11/16	Invalided to U.K.
85238	,,	Bullock, C. L.	Myrtle House, Brook Lane, Dumpesby, Cheshire.	1/ 1/17—30/ 1/17	,, ,,
89683	,,	*Burgess, E.	134, Houghton Road, Hetton-le-Hole, Durham.	15/ 1/18— 3/ 4/19	Posted to Army of Occupation.
160154	,,	Burgess, W.	16, High Street, Kinghorn, Fife, Scotland.	April '18— 9/ 2/19	Demobilised.
178332	,,	Burrage, C.	6, Pries Place, Horsham, Sussex.	22/ 4/18—30/ 6/18	To Hospital.
139726	,,	Butler, H. W.	Hillside, Lawston, Cambridge.	13/ 8/17— 3/ 4/19	Posted to Army of Occupation.
63668	,,	Bye, G. F.	106, High Street, Chesterton, Cambridge.	April '18—24/ 6/19	Demobilised with Cadre.
127177	,,	Cahill, P.	7, John Street, Drogheda, Ireland.	13/10/18—27/11/18	To Hospital.

No.	Rank	Name	Address	Dates	Remarks
49734	Gnr.	†Caddick, B.	31, Temple Street, Bilston, South Staffs.	13 8/17—26/10/17	Killed in action.
89687	,,	*Cage, C.	c/o G. Clarke, Esq., Needham Road, Harleston, Norfolk.	15/ 1/18— 3/ 4/19	Posted to Army of Occupation.
136612	,,	*Cameron, G.	Thornhill House, Hart Lane, West Hartlepool.	15/ 1/18— 9/ 2/18	To Hospital.
63730	,,	Cameron, S.	Longbridge Muir, Ruthwell, Dumfries.	30/ 5/17—21/ 3/18	,, ,,
185637	,,	*Campbell, A.	19, Meadow Park Street, Dennistoun, Glasgow.	15/ 1/18—24/ 6/19	Demobilised.
91637	,,	‡Campbell, W.	148, Dundee Street, Edinburgh	2/ 3/17—June, '17	Killed in action.
80992	,,	‡Cason, F.	Rye Hall, Eye, Suffolk.	4/ 9/16—10/ 7/17	Died of wounds.
65063	Sig.	Cathie, H. R.	31, Bruntsfield Avenue, Edinburgh.	19/10/16—13/ 5/19	Posted to Army of Occupation.
60513	Gnr.	Chandler, W.	42, Holly Road, Aldershot.	22/ 4/18—19/10/18	Invalided to U.K. (accidental injury).
69266	Sig.	Chapman, E. L.	2, Cumberland Road, West Cliff, Ramsgate.	7/ 4/17—Feb. '19	Posted to Base Commandant, Etaples.
152732	Gnr.	Chapman, W. A.	18, Reed Street, Govan, Glasgow.	13/ 8/17— 2/ 2/19	Demobilised.
111663	,,	Chant, S.	26, Tresco Road, Peckham Rye.	13/10/18—18/12/18	Demobilised while on leave in U.K.

* From 190 Siege Battery (Jan. 1918).   † Killed in action, or died of wounds or from other causes

REGTL. NO.	RANK.	NAME.	ADDRESS.	PERIOD OF SERVICE.	NATURE OF CASUALTY.
166868	Gnr.	Child, G. F.	21, Lowbank Street, Farsley, near Leeds.	22/ 4/18—22/12/18	Demobilised.
91693	,,	Coates, J. W.	High Street, Coleshill, Warwickshire.	7/12/16— 4/ 4/17	Invalided to U.K.
89595	,,	*Cockerham, R.	39, Watson Street, Burton-on-Trent.	15/ 1/18— 3/ 4/19	Posted to Army of Occupation.
21588	Sig	Coleman, J.	39, Evans Street, Crewe, Cheshire.	13/ 8/17— 4/ 1/19	Demobilised.
69833	Gnr.	Coles, H.	Shenington, near Banbury, Oxford.	30/ 9/18— 1/ 2/19	,,
153786	,,	Cooper, A.	St. Austins, Dulwich Village, London, S.E. 21.	13/10/18—21/12/18	Demobilised while on leave in U.K.
199257	,,	Corrie, R.	1, Belgarth Road, Newton, Carlisle.	19/ 9/18—Aug. '19	Demobilised with Equipment Guard.
57833	,,	Cove, A. R.	49, Chelmsford Road, Walthamstow.	22/ 4/18—28/ 9/18	Invalided to U.K.
32734	,,	†Cox, A. H.	7, Little John Street, Hoxton, London, N.	20/ 3/17—12/ 7/17	Killed in action.
175822	,,	Cooper, P.	10, Swan Street, Loughborough, Leicestershire.	6/ 3/18—18/ 4/18	To Hospital.
157012	,,	Cross, W.	35, Brookdene Road, Plumstead, S.E. 18.	13/ 8/17— 2/12/18	,, ,,

No.	Rank	Name	Address	Date	Remarks
188829	Gnr.	Cupit, S.	88, Stretton Row, near Alfreton, Derbyshire.	22/ 4/18—23/12/18	Demobilised.
147	„	Daubney, C. E.	57, Perth Street, Hull.	4/12/16—18/ 4/17	Invalided to U.K.
85729	„	Davies, F.	21, Elderton Road, Lower Sydenham.	4/ 9/16—Nov. '16	„ „
169436	„	*Dawes, E.	Merrow, Guildford, Surrey.	15/ 1/18—26/ 1/19	Demobilised.
78709	„	Dennant, W.	34, Norfolk Road, Essex Road, London, N.	24/ 2/17— 2/ 4/18	To Hospital.
83846	„	Dickinson, G. H.	43, Moor Street, Lincoln.	4/ 9/16— 3/ 4/19	Posted to Army of Occupation.
181475	„	Dixon, A. W.	Half-way Cottage, Walston Road, Commersdale, Carlisle.	30/ 9/18—Feb. '19	To Hospital.
70644	„	Dixon, R.	44, Linghedge Street, Battersea.	24/ 7/16—14/11/16	Invalided to U.K.
86583	Sig.	Dolby, H., MM.	Clapthorn, Lower Oundle, Northants.	4/ 9/16— 4/11/18	„ „
155833	Gnr.	Donohue, J.	28, Great Mersey Street, Commercial Street, Kirkdale, Liverpool.	13/ 8/17—19/ 2/19	To Hospital.
130418	„	‡Dorrington, W. A.	8, Mayfield Road, Brimsdown, Enfield, London, N.	13/ 8/17—20/ 8/17	Killed in action.
67010	„	*Duke, F.	1, Iris Cottage, Worcester Park, Surrey.	15/ 1/18— 6/12/18	To Hospital.

* From 190 Siege Battery (Jan. 1918).   ‡ Killed in action, or died of wounds or from other causes.

REGTL. NO.	RANK.	NAME.	ADDRESS.	PERIOD OF SERVICE.	NATURE OF CASUALTY.
110225	Gnr.	Durk, S. H.	87, Prince Edward Street, Crosshill, Glasgow.	20/ 3/17— 8/ 1/19	Demobilised.
91810	"	Dymond, A. C.	Brayford, near South Malden, N. Devon.	4/12/16—30/ 3/17	Invalided to U.K.
7721	"	Eales, G. C.	8, Margravine Road, Hammersmith, London.	21/11/16—11/ 7/17	To Hospital.
215148	"	Eames, J.	6, Cromwell Street, Thornhill Lees, Dewsbury.	19/ 9/18—20/10/18	Invalided to U.K. (accidental injury).
17891	"	Easley, E.	24, Skelbrook, Earlsfield.	4/12/16— 9/ 3/17	Transferred to Transportation Depot R.E.
119627	"	Edwards, C. W.	11, Horder Road, Fulham, London, S.W. 6.	13/ 8/17— 1/10/18	Invalided to U.K.
99850	"	*Eggleston, S.	South Farrington Farm, near Sunderland.	15/ 1/18— 8/ 2/19	Demobilised.
80345	"	Elsmore, A. H.	7A, Corporation Street, Stafford.	22/ 4/18—15/ 4/19	Posted to Army of Occupation.
84669	"	Entwistle, J. J.	88, Layton Lane, Blackpool.	13/ 8/17—27/ 7/19	Demobilised.
157047	"	Field, A.	3, Picton Street, Brighton.	13/ 8/17—Aug. '19	Demobilised with Equipment Guard.

No.	Rank	Name	Address	Dates	Remarks
76011	Gnr.	*Flack, H. J.	47, Hanover Buildings, London, S.E.	15/ 1/18—24/ 6/19	Demobilised with Cadre.
89558	,,	Fones, J.	48, High Park Road, Smethwick.	22/ 4/16— 5/ 7/18	To Hospital.
22122	,,	Forrest, J.	166, Govanhill Street, Govanhill, Glasgow.	30/ 9/18—24/ 6/19	Demobilised with Cadre.
282508	,,	Fowlis, H.	Rose Villa, St. Andrews, Scotland.	8/ 2/17— 5/ 8/18	To Hospital.
34666	,,	Francis, C.	11, George Street, Nottingham.	27/ 5/17— 9/ 8/18	To Hospital.
87176	Ftr./Gnr.	‡Freeman, F. T.	(Wife) Tadley Hill, near Basingstoke, Hants.	24/ 2/17—16/ 9/17	Died of wounds.
199011	Gnr.	Fricker, C. F.	Crenva House, Penalton, Ystrad-Mynach, Glam.	13/10/18—23/12/18	Demobilised.
59488	,,	Fuller, C. W.	Hobney Cottage, Pevensey, Sussex.	30/ 9/18—26/ 1/19	,,
317187	,,	Furness, H.	2, North Cottages, Farnham Royal, Slough.	6/ 3/18— 5/ 3/19	Posted to Army of Occupation.
117426	Sig.	Garbutt, W. T.	Thornton-le-Dale, Yorks.	30/ 7/18— 2/10/18	Invalided to U.K.
85854	Gnr.	Gardner, R.	46, Market Street, Northampton.	2/ 7/17—16/ 5/18	,, ,,
51187	Sig.	Garner, H. C.	153, Culcheth Lane, Newton Heath, Manchester.	24/ 9/16— 3/ 2/19	Demobilised.
177495	Gnr.	‡Gaston, W. J.	Newick Green, near Lewes, Sussex.	24/11/17— 5/ 4/18	Died of wounds.

* From 180 Siege Battery (Jan. 1918). ‡ Killed in action, or died of wounds or from other causes.

Regtl. No.	Rank.	Name.	Address.	Period of Service.	Nature of Casualty.
161686	Gnr.	Gatrell, F.	53, Station Road, Shepherd's Bush, London, W. 12.	6/ 3/18—13/ 5/19	Posted to Army of Occupation.
119048	,,	Glue, J.	Wood Cottage, Crown Pits Hill, Godalming, Surrey.	24/ 9/16—21/ 9/18	To Hospital.
156551	,,	Gocher, E. A.	5, Rectory Road, Stoke Newington, London.	26/ 4/18—Aug. '19	Demobilised with Equipment Guard.
177598	,,	Grant, P.	Sleevenagriddle, Downpatrick, Ireland.	24/ 11/17— 3/ 4/19	Posted to Army of Occupation.
167903	,,	*Green, F. J.	Park Farm, West Hedgeley, Warwickshire.	15/ 1/18—10/ 6/18	Invalided to U.K.
132816	,,	Griffin, H. P.	36, Lodge Lane, Liverpool.	19/ 4/17— 2/ 7/17	,, ,,
28833	,,	Hailes, R.	5, Sawmills Street, Capawell, Cork.	6/ 7/17—24/ 6/19	Demobilised with Cadre.
285007	,,	Hall, H.	Post Office, Hampstead Marshall, Newbury, Berks.	6/ 3/18—13/ 5/19	Posted to Army of Occupation.
59791	,,	Harding, C.	178, Alcester Street, Birmingham.	14/ 6/16—28/ 6/16	Invalided to U.K., 18/1/17.

No.	Rank	Name	Address	Dates	Remarks
47074	Gnr.	Hare, G. W.	25, Fanshaw Street, Newtown, South Hants.	24/ 9/16—18/ 1/17	Invalided to U.K., 18/1/17.
57042	,,	Harney, G.	7, Hope Street, Gorton, Manchester.	June, '16—14/ 6/16	Invalided to U.K.
136623	,,	*Hartley, T. H.	41, Burbank Street, West Hartlepool.	15/ 1/18— 3/ 1/19	Demobilised.
27157	,,	Harris, A.	St. Pauls Lodge, Kings Avenue, Winchmore Hill, London.	24/ 9/16— 8/12/18	Invalided to U.K.
32652I	Ftr./Gnr.	Harper, P. N.	Hope-a-Field, Dunoon, Argyll, Scotland.	12/ 4/18— 8/ 2/19	Demobilised.
124114	Gnr.	Harrison, F. G.	2, Hatfield Road, West Ealing, W. 13.	13/10/18—23/12/18	,,
138201	,,	Hartshorn, W. B.	3, Blackmarlow Street, Blyth.	15/ 1/18—23/12/18	,,
186462	Sig.	Haydock, W. W.	29A, Brook Street, Chorley, Lancs.	23/ 7/18—23/10/18	To Hospital.
91786	Gnr.	Haydon, A. J.	8, Gasking Street, Plymouth.	2/ 3/17— 4/ 9/18	,,
171803	,,	*Henshall, J. A.	18, Deakons Road, Wharton, Winsford, Cheshire.	15/ 1/18— 4/ 5/18	,,
146974	,,	Henson, G. S.	622, Gladstone Street, Peterborough.	3/ 7/18—31/ 7/18	,,
139453	Sig.	Hibbs, W. S.	14, Kensington Road, Steeple Hill, nr. Bristol.	6/ 7/17—13/ 5/19	Posted to Army of Occupation.

* From 190 Siege Battery (Jan. 1918).

REGTL. NO.	NAME.	RANK.	ADDRESS.	PERIOD OF SERVICE.	NATURE OF CASUALTY.
53718	Hilton, H.	Gnr.	Ciss Green, Hale, near Liverpool.	23/ 4/18—28/ 1/19	Demobilised.
119886	Hillier, G.	,,	Lyelands Farm, Bolney, near Haywards Heath, Sussex.	2/ 3/17—10/ 5/18	Posted to III. Corps H.A.
70430	Holloway, J.	,,	12, Crabtree Lane, Fulham Palace Rd., London	24/ 9/16—Jan. '17	Invalided to U.K.
374137	Holman, E.	,,	13, Woburn Place, Brighton.	22/ 4/18—24/ 6/19	Demobilised with Cadre.
1108	†Holmes, W.	,,	10, Ordnance Road, St. Johns Wood, N.W.	14/ 6/16—20/ 2/17	Killed in action.
58274	†Holtham, W. F.	,,	(Mother) 57, Winkfield Road, Wood Green, London, N.	24/ 2/17— 4/ 4/17	Died of wounds (burns).
121801	Hoopel, F.	,,	7, Loveridge Road, West Hampstead.	24/ 9/16—June, '17	To Hospital.
340294	Hornsby, A.	,,	8, West Street, South Queen Street, Morley.	22/ 4/18— 4/ 8/18	,, ,,
282613	Horsburgh, J.	,,	20, Fountain Place, Lonhead, Midlothian, Scotland.	22/ 4/18— 4/10/18	Invalided to U.K.
180476	*Howarth, H.	,,	117A, Bramstone Road, Burton-on-Trent.	15/ 1/18—29/12/18	Demobilised while on leave in U.K.

No.	Rank	Name	Address	Date	Remarks
12626	Gnr.	Howes, J.	20, Cwm Craig, Dowlais, South Wales.	2/ 3/17—27/ 7/17	Invalided to U.K.
111763	,,	*Humphreys, S.	12, Hudson Cottages, Artingborough.	15/ 1/18— 1/10/18	,, ,,
162894	,,	Humphreys, O. E.	52, Queens Hill, Newport (Mon.).	13/10/18—29/ 1/19	Demobilised.
29193	,,	Hunt, A. F.	212, Harborough Road, Kingsthorpe, Northants.	24/ 9/16—14/ 3/17	Invalided to U.K.
127321	,,	*Ibbotson, T.	22, Roberts Road, Doncaster.	15/ 1/18—16/11/18	To Hospital.
183983	,,	Ingram, B. A.	13, Swainscombe Terrace, Swanwark.	15/ 1/18—14/ 3/18	,, ,,
170781	,,	*Ings, E. W.	1, Moreland Road, Shirley, Southampton.	15/ 1/18—19/ 7/18	Posted to No. 2 O.M.W.
53538	,,	Jeffries, W. A.	62, Winston Street, Winston Green, Birmingham.	24/ 9/16— 2/ 3/17	To Hospital.
192352	,,	Jenkins, G.	22, Water Street, Neath, South Wales.	15/ 1/18—17/ 3/18	,, ,,
171378	,,	*Johnson, J.	126, Peasley Cross Lane, St. Helens, Lancs.	15/ 1/18—29/11/18	,, ,,
62114	,,	Jones, W.	30, Vicarage Road, Wolverhampton.	14/ 6/16—17/12/16	Attached to II. Corps H.A.
77941	,,	‡Kellett, H.	34, Southwell Street, Barnsley.	2/10/16—10/ 7/17	Killed in action.

* From 190 Siege Battery (Jan., 1918).   ‡ Killed in action, or died of wounds or from other causes.

Regtl. No.	Rank.	Name.	Address.	Period of Service.	Nature of Casualty.
114450	Gnr.	Kingdom, J. H.	6, Redlaver Street, Grangetown, Cardiff.	30/ 7/18— 1/10/18	Invalided to U.K.
19912	,,	Kirkwood, F. H.	37, Cumberland Street, Belle Ville, West Hartlepool.	2/ 3/17—14/ 4/17	To Hospital.
48466	,,	*Large, G. E.	365, Leigh Road, Atherton, near Manchester.	15/ 1/18—23/12/18	Demobilised.
70017	,,	*Last, A. W.	5, Richmond Park Road, Bournemouth.	15/ 1/18—25/ 3/18	Invalided to U.K
37138I	,,	*Lloyd, W.	Emporium, High Street, Fishguard.	15/ 1/18—24/ 6/19	Demobilised with Cadre.
293476	,,	Loveland, W.	12, Longdon Street, Bolton, Lancs.	23/10/16—April, '17	To Hospital.
57462	,,	*Lowrey, J.	Whitehaven, Cumberland.	15/ 1/18— 7/ 9/18	,, ,,
178953	Sig.	Luff, C.	66A, Gladesmore Road, Stamford Hill, London, N.	22/ 4/18—13/ 5/19	Posted to Army of Occupation.
139456	,,	Luker, A. E.	97, Hatherley Road, Gloucester.	6/ 7/17—13/ 5/19	Posted to Army of Occupation.
120252	Gnr.	*Lungley, H. J.	Near the Church, Wrabness, near Manningtree, Essex.	15/ 1/18—16/ 2/19	Demobilised.

190461	Sig.	Lye, S. W.	122, North Frederick Street, Glasgow.	24/ 8/18—30/10/18	To XIII. Corps H.A. Signals.
293474	Gnr.	Lyons, P.	Lismagen, Aughamora, co. Mayo, Ireland.	30/ 9/18—23/12/18	Demobilised.
98299	,,	Maden, J. K.	39, Reale Street, Littleborough, Lancs.	17/ 9/16—19/ 3/17	Invalided to U.K.
348201	,,	‡Maddocks, G. E.	21, High Street, Penarth, Glamorgan.	7/ 4/17—26/ 4/17	Died of wounds.
79369	,,	Maldrech, T.	Galle, Ceylon.	2/ 7/16— 9/11/16	Invalided to U.K.
160349	,,	Manning, C.	132, Harrogate Street, Undercliff, Bradford.	13/10/18— 5/ 3/19	Posted to Army of Occupation.
81158	,,	Marks, D.	13, Edwards Road, Bow, London.	24/ 9/16—29/ 9/16	To Hospital.
77095	,,	Martin, E.	27, Langton Street, Seedley, Salford, Manchester.	19/ 9/18—13/ 5/19	Posted to Army of Occupation.
98421	,,	McColm, A.	Sandhead, Stoney Kirk, Scotland.	14/ 1/17—13/ 7/17	Invalided to U.K.
1042	,,	McElone, P.	71, Lloyd Street, Middlesbrough.	16/10/16—22/ 1/17	To Hospital.
89737	,,	*Metcalf, M. T	Little Crakefield, Beadle, York.	15/ 1/18—16/ 2/19	Demobilised.
42715	,,	Middleton, A.	46, Hyde Street, Hyde, Deptford.	14/ 1/17—15/ 1/19	To U.K., to complete colour service.
61654	,,	‡Millen, F. W.	44, Tyers Street, Lambeth, London, S.E.	12/10/18— 2/11/18	Killed in action.

* From 190 Siege Battery (Jan. 1918).   ‡ Killed in action, or died of wounds or from other causes.

I

Regtl. No.	Rank.	Name.	Address.	Period of Service.	Nature of Casualty.
89688	Gnr.	*Mirfield, W.	12, Trafalgar Street, Batley, Yorks.	15/ 1/18—13/ 5/19	Posted to Army of Occupation.
188420	Sig.	Moseley, H.	27A, Commercial Street, Huddersfield.	23/ 4/18—Aug. '19	Demobilised with Equipment Guard.
92224	Gnr.	Moss, J.	8, Oxford Grove, Heavi-ley, Stockport.	17/ 9/16—19/12/18	Demobilised while on leave in U.K.
169598	Sig.	Moxon, E.	43, Squires End, Church End, Finchley.	26/ 4/18—30/ 5/18	To Hospital.
215710	Gnr.	Murray, D. E.	27, Hanbury Street, Pen-gam, Glamorgan.	3/10/18—29/11/18	,, ,,
80781	,,	Nelson, E.	12, Pelham Terrace, Pel-ham Street, Hull.	12/ 9/18—21/ 9/18	Invalided to U.K.
120135	,,	†Newby, J. A.	37, Cotterill Road, Sur-biton, Surrey.	30/ 5/17—15/ 8/17	Died of wounds.
31326	,,	Newell, E.	6, Arden Street, Wool-wich.	16/ 7/16—14/ 9/16	Invalided to U.K.
186078	Sig.	Oldham, E. M.	13, Vale Road, Reddish, Stockport, Lancs.	24/ 8/18—15/11/19	To Hospital.
52111	Gnr.	O'Keeffe, M.	Lacken-Roe, Glanmire, co. Cork.	28/10/18—24/ 6/19	Demobilised with Cadre.
105760	,,	Openshaw, F. W.	11, Heywood Street, South Bury, Lancs.	2/11/17—15/ 5/18	To Hospital.

No.	Rank	Name	Address	Date	Remarks
85377	Gnr.	Owen, R. J.	Pewgwyn, Nannerch, near Mold, South Wales.	28/ 7/17—18 9/18	To Hospital.
362435	,,	†Oliver, G. E.	5, Balls Road, East Birkenhead.	28/ 7/17—21/ 3/18	Died of wounds.
82895	,,	Palethorpe, A. T.	Little Houghton, Northampton.	19/10/16—Aug., 19	Demobilised with Equipment Guard.
83868	,,	Panting, R.	4, Stanley Avenue, Leslie Road, Nottingham.	19/10/16—13/ 5/19	Posted to Army of Occupation.
96261	,,	Perry, H. C.	1, Kinlock Street, Holloway, London, N.	9/10/16—31/ 1/17	Invalided to U.K.
46541	,,	*Philbrick, F.	279, Morland Road, East Croydon, London.	15/ 1/18—27/ 6/18	,, ,,
6878	,,	Pocock, J. A.	108, Central Street, Barrow-in-Furness.	19/10/16— 8/ 2/17	Posted to 45th H.A.G.
39891	,,	Posner, N.	74, Cleveland Street, Euston Road, London.	16/ 7/16—13/ 1/19	To U.K. to complete colour service.
86536	,,	Postle, R. G.	70, Bromley Road, Catford.	9/10/16—24/11/16	Invalided to U.K.
313166	,,	Preston, G.	63, Mount Pleasant, Shelton, Stoke-on-Trent.	15/ 4/17— 7/ 8/17	,, ,,
42412	,,	Price, J. L.	55, Avondale Road, Gelliystrad, Rhondda, Glam.	4/ 4/17—12/ 7/17	,, ,,
224625	,,	Quaile, R.	Carrick-on-Shannon, co. Leitrim, Ireland.	12/ 9/18—24/ 6/19	Demobilised with Cadre.

* From 190 Siege Battery (Jan. 1918).   ‡ Killed in action, or died of wounds or from other causes.

Regtl. No.	Rank.	Name.	Address.	Period of Service.	Nature of Casualty.
34829I	Gnr.	Randall, P.	137, City Road, Roath, Cardiff.	23/ 5/18—24/ 6/19	Demobilised with Cadre.
132440	,,	*Rigg, W.	9, New Row, Eldon, near Bishop Auckland, Durham.	15/ 1/18— 6/12/18	To Hospital.
30114	Sig.	Roberts, G.	Church End, Hanley Gate, Worcester.	2/ 7/16— 3/ 3/19	Re-enlisted.
285042	Gnr.	Roberts, W. T.	12, Tregonwell Road, Bournemouth.	13/ 8/17—29/ 7/18	To 139 H.B., R.G.A.
85781	,,	Robinson, F. E.	112, Chase Side, Old Southgate, London.	9/ 7/18—21/ 9/18	Invalided to U.K.
13664I	,,	*Robson, J. T.	42, Durham Street, Hartlepool.	15/ 1/18—27/12/18	Demobilised while on leave in U.K.
104000	,,	*Roe, E.	12, Surgery Street, Brow, Haworth, Yorks.	15/ 1/18— 3/ 4/19	Posted to Army of Occupation.
120456	,,	Rose, R. F.	"Live and Let Live" Inn, Watton, Norfolk.	15/ 4/17—16/ 7/17	Invalided to U.K.
104093	,,	*Ross, T.	182, Martin Street, Leicester.	15/ 1/18—23/ 4/18	,, ,,
209239	,,	Roust, W. B.	15, Cranham Road, Bermondsey, S.E.	30/ 9/18— 7/ 2/19	Demobilised.
14I447	,,	Rowley, W.	93, Cowersby Street, Moss Side, Manchester.	13/ 8/17—Aug. '19	Demobilised with Equipment Guard.

	Gnr.				
97750	Gnr.	‡Ryder, R.	19, Harrogate Street, Wigan, Lancs.	20/11/16—12/ 8/17	Killed in action.
206314	,,	‡Seargeant, J. W.	Thornton Street, Barrow-on-Humber, Lincs.	19/ 9/18— 7/10/18	Died of wounds.
308600	,,	Saunders, A. N.	78, Parkhill Road, Dingle, Liverpool.	15/ 4/17—28/ 7/17	To Hospital.
109148	,,	‡Schnaar, C. H.	34, Whitchen Street, New Cross, London.	4/ 4/17—24/ 5/18	Killed in action.
296709	,,	Scott, A. G.	27, Leigh Road, Leyton.	4/ 4/17—24/ 6/19	Demobilised with Cadre.
114226	,,	Schumann, A.	14, Chester Place, Liverpool.	6/ 3/18— 5/ 1/19	Demobilised while on leave in U.K.
170062	,,	*Shenton, W.	Haughton, near Stafford.	15/ 1/18—15/ 4/19	Posted to Army of Occupation.
329634	,,	Sheppard, A. C.	Well Street, Paignton, S. Devon.	13/ 8/17—24/ 6/19	Demobilised with Cadre.
99248	,,	Singleton, R.	32, Bremister Road, Winton, Bournemouth.	6/ 3/18—19/ 2/19	To Hospital.
313666	,,	Smith, F. R.	New Road, Anesby, Leicester.	6/ 3/18—30/12/18	Demobilised.
170465	,,	Smith, H.	Frempton, Cotterell, Bristol.	6/ 3/18— 5/ 4/18	To Hospital.
76249	,,	Stevens, F.	53, Palmerston Road, Wimbledon, S.W. 19.	23/ 2/18— 1/11/18	,, ,,
179417	,,	Stroud, T.	33, Grayland Road, Peckham, London.	30/ 9/18—21/ 1/19	Demobilised.

* From 190 Siege Battery (Jan. 1918).   ‡ Killed in action, or died of wounds or from other causes.

REGTL. NO.	RANK.	NAME.	ADDRESS.	PERIOD OF SERVICE.	NATURE OF CASUALTY.
87436	Gnr.	Taylor, A.	Steepleton Cottages, Stockbridge, Hants.	4/ 4/17—18/ 6/17	Demobilised.
119824	„	Taylor, F.	7, Skinner Street, Chatham.	15/ 4/17—14/10/17	„
127946	„	Taylor, F. A.	55, Richmond Road, Ipswich.	13/ 8/17—25/ 6/18	To Hospital.
89702	„	Taylor, G.	22, Station Road, Earl Shilton, Leicester.	3/10/18— 3/ 2/19	To Hospital (accidental injury).
179903	„	Thornburrow, J.	56, Darcy Street, Workington, Cumberland.	12/ 9/18—23/12/18	Demobilised.
174216	„	*Treleaven, F. G.	Hensaviston, High Street, nr. St. Austell, Cornwall	15/ 1/18— 7/10/18	To Hospital (accidental injury).
157522	F/.Gnr.	Tugby, J.	Alga House, Swinton, Yorks.	23/ 5/18—21/ 1/19	To Hospital.
94272	Gnr.	*Wade, J. W.	Garden House, Cross Gate Moor, Durham.	15/ 1/18—15/ 4/19	Posted to Army of Occupation.
96312	Sig.	Wade, S.	104, Cannon Street, Bury St. Edmunds, Suffolk.	28/ 2/18—29/ 7/18	To Hospital.
83858	Gnr.	*Walker, J. A.	Foxes Lodge, Marchington, near Uttoxeter, Staffs.	15/ 1/18—13/ 5/19	Posted to Army of Occupation.
71639	„	Wallace, W. C.	Stanton Street, Quinton, nr. Chippenham, Wilts.	7/12/16—26/ 8/17	To Hospital.

161389	Gnr.	Waltho, T. F.	Fair View, Llangollen, N. Wales.	6/ 3/18— 5/ 1/19	Demobilised while on leave in U.K.
92057	,,	Warburton, A. B.	1, Buxton Road, Stockport, Cheshire.	27/ 4/18—Aug. '19	Demobilised with Equipment Guard.
136652	,,	*Waterman, J.	10, William Street, West Hartlepool.	15/ 1/18—28/12/18	Demobilised while on leave in U.K.
163460	,,	Watson, A.	406, Cumberland Street, Glasgow, Scotland.	23/ 5/18— 7/ 1/19	Demobilised.
146485	,,	‡Wayman, H. O.	St. Aubyns, Robin Hood Lane, Sutton, Surrey.	15/ 8/17—29/10/17	Died of wounds.
322261	,,	Welfare, A. J.	Sundridge Hill Farm, Knockholt, Sevenoaks, Kent.	3/10/18—Aug. '19	Demobilised with Equipment Guard.
196021	Wh./Gnr.	*White, A.	Greenend, Kingsthorpe, Northants.	15/ 1/18—24/ 6/19	Demobilised with Cadre.
173980	Gnr.	White, G. E.	1, Cranberry Road, Fulham, London, S.W.	23/10/16—19/12/16	Invalided to U.K.
177921	Sig.	White, F. J.	54, Selborne Road, Southgate, London, N. 14.	6/ 3/18—10/ 1/19	Demobilised.
192306	Gnr.	White, G. A.	Simon Street, Alderney, Channel Islands.	3/10/18— 4/ 1/19	Demobilised while on leave in U.K.
167447	Sig.	White, J. E.	57, Westfield Road, Bradford, Yorks.	26/ 4/18—27/ 5/19	Posted to Army of Occupation.
88463	Gnr.	Whitfield, A.	8, de Bouvier Crescent, Whitmore Road, Hackney.	27/ 4/18— 3/ 4/19	Posted to Army of Occupation.

* From 190 Siege Battery (Jan. 1918). ‡ Killed in action, or died of wounds or from other causes.

135

REGTL. NO.	NAME.	RANK.	ADDRESS.	PERIOD OF SERVICE.	NATURE OF CASUALTY.
106814	Wilband, E. E.	Gnr.	70, Bathampton Road, Bath.	19/ 9/18—27/ 5/19	Posted to Army of Occupation.
326158	Wilcox, C.	,,	7, Myrtle Square, Mean-wood, Leeds.	19/ 9/18— 3/ 3/19	Posted to XIII. Corps H.A.
286559	Wilkinson, E.	Sig.	15, Bolehill Lane, Crookes, Sheffield.	28/ 2/18— 1/ 8/18	To Hospital.
171929	Wilkinson, H. C.	Gnr.	The Lodge, Higher Heys-ham, Morecambe,Lancs.	28/ 2/18—12/ 4/18	Invalided to U.K.
88471	Williams, J. A.	,,	4, Delverton Road, Wal-worth, London.	13/ 8/17— 1/10/18	,, ,,
321525	*Williams, W. J.	,,	Melvern,Claremont Road, Redruth, Cornwall.	15/ 1/18—28/ 9/18	Invalided to U.K. (accidental in-jury).
176492	Willis, J. T.	,,	15, Budwith Road, Bright Side, Sheffield.	28/ 2/18—24/ 3/18	Invalided to U.K.
338763	Willis, T. C.	,,	2, Liddles Terrace, West Sleekburn, Chopping-ton, Northumberland.	6/ 3/18—24/ 6/19	Demobilised with Cadre.
117207	Wilson, J.	,,	92, Bankhead Road,Bank-head, Aberdeen.	15/ 4/17—10/12/17	To Hospital.
113976	Wilson, G.	,,	105, Upper Bond Street, Hinckley, Leicester-shire.	July '17—Aug. '19	Demobilised with Equipment Guard.

136

Number	Rank	Name	Address	Dates	Remarks
167088	Gnr.	Wilson, G. T.	Townhead, Halton, Staffs.	6/ 3/18—13/ 4/18	To Hospital.
73158	,,	Wilson, G. Y.	Oathlew, Forfar, Scotland.	21/ 4/18—13/ 5/19	Posted to Army of Occupation.
18048I	,,	*Windle, T.	25, Queen Victoria Road, Burnley.	15/ 1/18—29/12/18	Demobilised.
338507	,,	Wisdom, J. F.	3, The Chain, Sandwich, Kent.	3/10/18—24/ 6/19	Demobilised with Cadre.
97418	Sig.	Woar, T.	Stone Cottage, Fishwick, near Preston.	23/10/16—28/ 9/18	Invalided to U.K.
275327	Gnr.	*Wood, J.	143, Malden Road, Kentish Town, London.	15/ 1/18—24/ 6/19	Demobilised with Cadre.
175654	,,	Woodhouse, T.	13, Bamfield Street, Langsett Road, Sheffield.	27/ 4/18— 5/10/18	To Hospital.
181919	,,	Woodman, A. G.	25, Carlisle Road, Green Bank, Bristol.	28/ 2/18—23/ 4/18	,, ,,
161054	,,	Wright, T.	19, Ashton Street, Blackburn.	23/ 7/18—23/12/18	Demobilised.
167492	,,	Yates, A.	2, Alexandra Road, Burnley, Leeds.	6/ 3/18—24/ 2/19	,,
91443	,,	Yeo, A.	Sea View, Mortehoe, N. Devon.	27/11/16—23/ 2/17	To Hospital.

* From 190 Siege Battery (Jan. 1918).

ATTACHED TO 94 S.B.

REGTL. NO.	RANK.	NAME.	ADDRESS.	PERIOD OF SERVICE.	NATURE OF CASUALTY.
	R.A.F.				
103297	2/A.M.	Chapman, E.	9, Bonnie Brow, Rhodes, Manchester.	14/3/18—Jan. '19	Rejoined R.A.F.
63135	,,	Caddick, W. G.	40, Furness Road, Bow, London.	— Oct. '18.	Transferred (since died).
6891	1/A.M.	Sheward, C. J.	5, Ashcroft Road, Cirencester, Gloucester.	1/10/16—29/ 6/18	Transferred to Balloon Section.
	2/A.M.	Williams.	—	—	—
CZ/8240	Tel.	Yule, J. (R.N.R.)	56, Barnes Street, White Crook, Clydebank, N.B.	26/11/17—10/ 3/18	Demobilised.
	R.A.O.C.				
1110	A./S./Sgt.	*King, G. W.	101, Glenparke Road, Forest Gate, Essex.	30/ 5/16—Nov. '17	Posted Ordnance Mobile Workshops.
T./13111	,,	Taylor, H. P.	289, Clarendon Park Road, Leicester.	Nov. '17—31/ 7/18	Transferred to Base Workshops.
T./837	,,	Wheeler, H. S. T.	Rockwood House, Hanham Abbots, near Bristol.	29/ 7/18—19/ 5/19	Posted to I.C.S. Caudry.

* Original Unit.

PART VII.

NOMINAL ROLL OF R.A.S.C. (M.T.) (ATTACHED).

(ARRANGED IN CHRONOLOGICAL ORDER.)

(1) OFFICERS.

RANK.	NAME.	PERIOD WITH UNIT.		HOME ADDRESS.	REMARKS.
		FROM	TO		
2nd Lt. (since Lt.)	Dunn, R. T.	28/5/16	16/8/16	c/o Sir Charles R. Mc-Grigor, Bart., & Co., Bankers, Panton Street, London, W.	Posted to 143 S.B.
2nd Lt. (since Lt.)	Parker, E.	May, 1916	10/8/16	c/o Sir Charles R. Mc-Grigor, Bart., & Co., Bankers, Panton Street, London, W.	Posted to 54th Div. Supply Column.
2nd Lt. (since Lt.)	Kemp-Scriven, R. S.	Aug., 1916	Feb., 1917	c/o Sir Charles R. Mc-Grigor, Bart., & Co., Bankers, Panton Street, London, W.	Evacuated to U.K. (Trench Fever).
2nd Lt. (since Lt.)	Ware, R. G.	16/8/16	3/11/16	Barrow Castle, Bath.	Posted to 62 S.B.
2nd Lt. (since Lt.)	Biscoe, A. F.	Nov., 1916	May, 1917	Next of kin, Mrs. V. Biscoe, Dee Bank, Corwen, N. Wales.	Since died (22/2/19, Cologne—Pneumonia).

Rank.	Name.	Period with Unit.		Home Address.	Remarks.
		From	To		
2nd Lt. (since Capt.)	Watkin, W. C.	9/3/17	5/5/17	70, Crescent Road, Wood Green, London.	Posted to " E " Siege Park.
Lieut.	Brooke-Alder, B.	May, 1917	Sept., 1917	Redholm, Esher, Surrey.	Invalided while on leave in U.K.
2nd Lt. (since Lt.)	Dobson, H. D.	July, 1917	Aug., 1917	15, Nevern Mansions, Earls Court, London.	Posted to " O " Siege Park.
2nd Lt. (since Lt.)	Reynolds, J. F. C., M.C.	10/11/17	8/6/18	56, Woodstock Road, Golders Green, N.W.4.	Posted to M.T. Inspection Branch.
2nd Lt.	Prior, S. C.	Jan., 1918	16/4/18	Burman Road, Shirley, near Birmingham.	Invalided to U.K. Concussion.
2nd Lt. (since Lt.)	Parish, J. E.	June, 1918	Sept., 1918	14, Copeland Road, Walthamstow, Essex.	Posted to 41 S.B.
Lieut.	Smith, N. S.	June, 1918	Sept., 1918	—	Posted to " C " S.A.P. Workshops (since died).
Lieut.	Harrison, T. V.	24/9/18	June, 1919	" The Priory," Alcester, Warwickshire.	Volunteered for Army of Occupation.

REGTL. No.	RANK.	NAME.	HOME ADDRESS.	PERIOD OF SERVICE WITH 94 SIEGE BATTERY.		NATURE OF CASUALTY.
				FROM	TO	
M2/152953	Sgt.	Elliott, J. W.	728, Dundas Street, London, Ontario, Canada.	22/8/16	17/12/18	Evacuated Sick to England.
M2/098485	,,	Peach, S. A.	149, Chatham Street, Old Kent Road, London, S.E.	3/11/17	16/3/18	Transferred to 5th Cavalry, S.A.P. Reserve Pool.
M/21292	,,	Pixton, I.	10, Monk Street, Warwick.	15/1/18	1919	Eligible for Demobilisation. Regular Soldier, time expired.
M2/049177	,,	†Smith, P. W.	11, Heriot Hall Terrace, Edinburgh.	22/8/16	16/5/18	Evacuated Sick.
M2/152512	,,	†Burslem, R.	c/o R. Waywell, Cornbrook, Manchester.	21/6/18	29/1/19	Demobilised.
DM2/195053	Cpl.	†Adams, W. F., M.M.	2, Old London Road, Hastings.	15/1/18	1919	Eligible for Demobilisation.
DM2/154903	,,	Allum, H. W. W.	52, Clifford Gardens, Willesden, N.W.	15/1/18	25/9/18	Transferred to 156 S.B.A.C.

N.B.—No man who did not serve in the Battery Ammunition Column during January 18th or afterwards (on formation of 6-gun Battery) is included in this Roll, previous records having been destroyed. † Caterpillar Section.

Regtl. No.	Rank.	Name.	Home Address.	Period of Service with 94 Siege Battery. From	To	Nature of Casualty.
M2/166353	Cpl.	Ayres, W. F.	The Square, Bloxham, nr. Banbury, Oxon.	25/9/18	27/11/18	Transferred to 355 S.B.A.C.
M2/034487	,,	Bowles, A.	308, Bramford Road, Ipswich.	22/8/16	10/4/18	Transferred to
M2/194479	,,	Bridge, C. G.	39, Hatfield Road, Ipswich.	22/8/16	1/6/18	Transferred to 327 S.B.A.C., then 504 S.B.A.C.
M2/202508	,,	Bundock, W. J.	39, Mansfield Road, Exeter.	15/1/18	1919	Eligible for Demobilisation.
M2/046302	,,	Clark, P. C.	130, Belsize Road, S. Hampstead, N.W.	3/11/17	1919	Eligible for Demobilisation.
MS/4134	,,	Cole, G. A.	Hillside Cottage, Kenley, Surrey.	22/8/16	17/11/18	Transferred to 355 S.B.A.C.
M1/07550	,,	Craig, A. B.	2, Royal Cottages, Cookham Dean, Berks.	22/8/16	16/12/18	Evacuated Sick.
DM2/096639	,,	Hargreaves, J.	21, St. Paul Street, Low Moor, Clitheroe, Lancs.	15/1/18	1919	Eligible for Demobilisation.
DM2/177957	,,	†Harrington, C. H.	Berwerdy Terrace, Pontypridd.	15/1/18	1919	Eligible for Demobilisation.

M2/147879	Cpl.	Liley, W. H.	Norfolk Arms, Roffey, Horsham, Sussex.	15/1/18	24/8/18	Evacuated Sick.
M1/5936	,,	Reynolds, S. L.	63, Cheltenham Street, Malvern, Adelaide, S. Australia.	6/6/18	31/1/19	Demobilised.
M2/167966	,,	†Smith, H. C., M.M.	Old Bell Cottage, Luton Road, Harpenden.	22/8/16	13/12/18	,,
M2/12093	,,	Thomas, C. G.	10, Croft Road, Cowbridge, S. Wales.	15/1/18	2/7/18	Evacuated (Accident).
DM2/206799	L./Cpl.	*Crumpton, H.	7, Wellington Road, Woolwich.	15/1/18	17/11/18	Transferred to 41 S.B.A.C. (died 1/12/18) (Sickness)
MS/926	,,	Dowman, T.	64, Glasgow Road, Rutherglen, Glasgow.	22/8/18	6/6/18	Transferred to 227 S.B.A.C.
M2/175508	,,	Golding, M. J.	130, Weedington Road, Kentish Town, N.W.	22/8/16	8/3/19	Transferred to 70 S.B.A.C.
M2/174731	,,	†Green, W. S.	40, Burdett Road, Bow, London, E.	22/8/16	15/7/18	Evacuated to Base.
DM2/180334	,,	*†Jones, E. H.	Penylryn Halkyn, N. Wales.	15/1/18	26/2/19	Died in Hospital (Sickness).
M2/019349	,,	Eccles, J.	45, Spring Lane, Radcliffe, Lancs.	22/8/16	7/1/18	Demobilised.
DM2/190887	,,	Mills, T. H.	213, Spring Vale Road, Sheffield.	15/1/18	15/1/19	,,

* Killed. or died of wounds, or sickness.   † Caterpillar Section.

Regtl. No.	Rank.	Name.	Home Address.	Period of Service with 94 Siege Battery. From	Period of Service with 94 Siege Battery. To	Nature of Casualty.
M2/174574	L./Cpl.	†Phillips, W. D.	12, Colberg Road, Wood Green, London, N.	22/8/16	8/3/19	Transferred to 70 S.B.A.C.
M2/121104	,,	Williams, A. R.	154, High Street, Lewes, Sussex.	4/9/16	17/11/18	Transferred to 355 S.B.A.C.
M/33103	,,	Woolsgrove, J. H.	124, Campden House, Kensington, W.	15/1/18	17/11/18	Transferred to 355 S.B.A.C.
M2/222161	,,	Wood, F.	6, Bormwich Road, Worcester.		8/3/19	Transferred to 70 S.B.A.C.
DM2/206578	Pte.	Allen, A. C.	15, Tetcott Street, Kings Road, Chelsea, S.W.	15/1/18	12/4/18	Transferred to 41 S.B.A.C.
DM2/178618	,,	Allum, H. J. W.	23, Richboro' Road, Cricklewood, London, N.W.	15/1/18	25/9/18	Transferred to 156 S.B.A.C.
DM2/189973	,,	Auty, P.	Woolmarket, Pontefract.	26/4/18	27/1/19	Demobilised.
M2/227571	,,	Bain, H.	Cairneywhyn Ramoir, Banchory, Aberdeenshire.	15/1/18	12/4/18	Transferred to 41 S.B.A.C.
M2/114845	,,	Baird, R.	33, Oldgate Street, Morpath.	22/8/16	23/12/18	Evacuated Sick.

DM2/190209	Pte.	Bennett, G. W.	Albert Road, Keynsham, Bristol.	15/1/18		Evacuated.
DM2/180185	,,	†Bennett, C. F., M.M.	12, St. Andrews Terrace, Dover.	15/1/18	8/3/19	Transferred to 70 S.B.A.C.
M2/180710	,,	Bowdrey, A. J.	3, Harley Mews, Marylebone, W.	15/1/18	25/2/18	Evacuated Wounded.
M2/194456	,,	Brunskill, F.	157, Hartlington Road, S. Lambeth.	22/8/16	23/11/18	Evacuated Sick.
M2/164539	,,	*Barefoot, O. J.	60, Charles Street, Iffley Road, Oxford.	22/8/16	16/11/18	Evacuated Sick. (since deceased—Sickness).
M2/200577	,,	Berry, H.	35, High Street, Halton, Leeds.	22/8/16	17/11/18	Transferred to 41 S.B.A.C.
M2/201095	,,	Bolger, J.	31, Baxter Street, Dundee.	22/8/16	1919	Eligible for Army of Occupation.
DM2/138405	,,	Bootle, J.	94, Walnot Street, Bethnal Green Road, N.E.	5/12/17	8/11/18	Evacuated Sick.
M2/167555	,,	†Bell, J. W.	Little Bampton, Wigton, Cumberland.	22/8/16	8/3/19	Transferred to 70 S.B.A.C.
DM2/170283	,,	*Brown, A.	18, Pattison Street, Dalmuir, Dumbartonshire.	22/8/16	6/10/18	Killed in action.
DM2/164718	,,	Burke, W.	13, Duncombe Street, Middlesbrough.	22/8/16	10/7/18	Evacuated Sick.
DM2/223775	,,	Bright, H.	12, Beresford St., Shelton, Stoke-on-Trent.	10/7/17	21/7/18	Transferred to Fourth Army T.S.

* Killed or died of wounds or sickness.　　† Caterpillar Section.

Regtl. No.	Rank.	Name.	Home Address.	Period of Service with 94 Siege Battery. From	To	Nature of Casualty.
M2/200722	Pte.	Branch, H. H.	26, Wood Street, Wellingborough.	27/7/17	25/9/18	Transferred to 1st Heavy Repair Workshop.
DM2/223767	,,	Brittain, W. E.	21, Relf Road, Peckham Rye, London, S.E.	15/1/18	23/7/18	Evacuated Sick.
M1/07244	,,	Brown, M. H.	5, Eastern Road, Brockley, London, S.E.	15/1/18	1/1/19	Transferred to " N" S.A.P., H.Q.
DM2/180095	,,	†Beabey, S. A.	4, Admiralty Road, Portsea, Portsmouth	15/1/18	6/7/18	Evacuated Sick.
M/225317	,,	Barrett, H.	44, Melgand Road, Holloway Road, London, N.	15/1/18	17/11/18	Transferred to 355 S.B.A.C.
M/375529	,,	Bishop, A.	1, Denton Road, Hooley Hill, Manchester.	7/8/18	1919	Retained in Army of Occupation.
M/297148	,,	Betts, E. A.	222, Colonial Road, Bordesley Green, Birmingham.	27/9/18	1919	Retained in Army of Occupation.

DM2/171584	Butler, C. J.	"	16, Isabella Street, Blackfriars Road, London, S.E.	15/1/18	1/6/18 (approx.)	Evacuated (Accident).
DM2/169585	Cleaver, F.	"	30, Walker St, Limehouse, London, E.	22/8/16	25/3/19	Demobilised.
DM2/206794	Conion, H.	"	62, Louis Street, Hull.	15/1/18	20/3/19	Evacuated Sick.
M2/175735	Coopland, R.	"	Warren Vale Farm, Normandale, Wadsley, Sheffield.	15/1/18	10/8/18	
M2/194451	Coton, F.	"	Club House, Brandon, Coventry.	22/8/16	22/11/18	"
M2/101741	Crayton, W. J.	"	147, Warwards Lane, Selly Park, Birmingham.	22/8/16	17/12/18	"
DM2/170305	Cox, A. A.	"	Lytchett Matravers, Poole, Dorset.	22/8/16	31/10/18	Evacuated Wounded.
M2/150857	†Cooper, H.	"	1, Walnut Street, Southport.	26/8/18	8/3/19	Transferred to 70 S.B.A.C.
M2/082744	Daunton, N. A.	"	100, Hockley Hill, Birmingham.	22/8/16	1919	Eligible for Demobilisation.
DM2/168557	Davies, G. G.	"	The Exchange, Llantwit-Vardre, Pontypridd.	22/8/16	1919	Eligible for Army of Occupation.
M2/047209	Drury, J.	"	266, Marboro' Road, Oxford.	15/11/16	1919	Eligible for Demobilisation.
M2/192218	Doolan, T. P.	"	2, Oakfield St., Bamber Bridge, Preston.	22/8/16	17/11/18	Transferred to 41 S.B.A.C.

† Caterpillar Section.

Regtl. No.	Rank.	Name.	Home Address.	Period of Service with 94 Siege Battery. From	To	Nature of Casualty.
M2/11346I	Pte.	Davis, R. F.	227B, Brooke Road, Upper Clapton, London, N.E.	1/5/17	1919	Retained in Army of Occupation.
M2/19404I	,,	Edwards, J. W.	12, Byron Street, London Road, Buxton, Derby.	15/11/16	17/11/18	Transferred to 327 S.B.A.C.
M2/27338I	,,	Evans, E. J.	2, Jones Yard, Fishpool Street, St. Albans.	15/1/18	17/7/18	Evacuated Sick.
M/352457	,,	Earthy, O. E.	5, Shipman Road, Forest Hill, London	5/4/18	17/11/18	Transferred to 41 S.B.A.C.
MI/05940	,,	Fell, P. W.	Bentcliffe Cross Bank, Urmston, Lancs.	22/8/16	15/12/18	Evacuated Sick.
DM2/164546	,,	Firby, W.	17, Fairford Terrace, Dewesbury Road, Leeds.	22/8/16	17/11/18	Transferred to 41 S.B.A.C.
M2/033118	,,	Funnell, E.	216, Cator Street, Peckham, London, S.E.	15/1/18	10/11/18	Evacuated Sick.
DM2/168377	,,	†Faulkner, H.	18, Horse Market, Northampton.	6/5/18	20/3/19	Demobilised.

M2/114249	,,	Fawdington, A. W.	6, Bewlay St., Bishopthorpe Road, York.	31/7/18	17/11/18	Transferred to 355 S.B.A.C.
M/304213	,,	Gerdes, R.	30, Gore Road, Hackney, London, N.E.	15/6/17	17/11/18	Transferred to 327 S.B.A.C.
M2/223619	,,	Hocper, C. H.	Fern Hill Heath, Worcester.	15/1/18	17/11/18	Transferred to 355 S.B.A.C.
M2/192373	,,	Honey, E. E.	Stanmer Park, Sussex.	22/8/16	1919	Retained in Army of Occupation.
M2/178501	,,	†Hughes, W. T.	Brawdy Mill, Penycwn, Pembrokeshire.	22/8/16	24/8/18	Evacuated Sick.
M2/167460	,,	†Hall, J.	Moss Road, Garstang, Lancs.	22/8/16	1/3/19	Evacuated Sick.
MS/4713	,,	Harwood, J.	123, Bucknall New Road, Hanley, Stoke.	25/12/17	1919	Retained in Army of Occupation.
M2/138438	,,	Hutton, O. F.	2, Gransdon Road, Wendle Park, Shepherds Bush.	15/6/17	1919	Eligible for Demobilisation.
M2/103429	,,	Iles, W.	10, Midd Vue, Bilton Lane, Harrogate.	10/11/17	17/11/18	Transferred to 41 S.B.A.C.
M2/193446	,,	James, A. W.	Glen-Rhos, King Street, Woolaston, Stourbridge.	22/8/16	1919	Retained in Army of Occupation.
MS/4776	,,	†Jones, N. A.	26, Oxford Road, Waterloo, Liverpool.	10/4/18	1919	Eligible for Demobilisation.
M2/230001	,,	Johnson, A.	16, Rochester Terrace, London, N.W.	9/10/18	1919	Eligible for Demobilisation.
M2/272496	,,	Kenning, H.	Clay Cross, Derbyshire.	15/1/18	7/4/18	Evacuated Wounded

† Caterpillar Section.

149

Regtl. No.	Rank.	Name.	Home Address.	Period of Service with 94 Siege Battery. From	Period of Service with 94 Siege Battery. To	Nature of Casualty.
M2/194464	Pte.	Littlewood, H.	21, Albion Street, Derby.	22/8/16	31/12/18	Demobilised.
DM2/165104	,,	Lewis, E. E.	14, Custellation Street, Roath, Cardiff.	25/11/16	1919	Retained in Army of Occupation.
M2/136751	,,	Lowing, W.	8, Hammonds Lane, Warley Road, Brentwood, Essex.	25/12/16	1919	Eligible for Demobilisation.
M2/114271	,,	Love, W.	238, Holybrook Street, Glasgow.	27/3/17	31/3/19	Demobilised.
M2/201418	,,	Lamport, W. J.	Park View, Upper Hythe, Farnham, Surrey.	30/7/18	24/12/18	Evacuated Sick.
M2/207794	,,	Martin, A. J.	190, Church Road, Stokingford, Nuneaton.	8/12/16	17/11/18	Transferred to 41 S.B.A.C.
M2/120735	,,	Marshall, A.	Burtons Land, Busby, Glasgow.	15/1/18	22/11/18	Evacuated Sick.
M4/03798i	,,	Munns, F.	Upper Halliford, nr. Shepperton, Middlesex.	15/1/18	27/11/18	,,

Number		Name	Address			Remarks
DM2/189404	,,	Mould, W.	Myrtle Bank, Hambleton Grove, Knaresborough.	25/11/16	1919	Eligible for Demobilisation.
M2/081940	,,	McLaren, G. D.	18, Henderson Terrace, Edinburgh.	15/11/16	17/11/18	Transferred to 355 S.B.A.C.
M2/181419	,,	Mackenzie, J. R.	9, Thomson Avenue, Johnstone.	15/7/16	24/11/18	Evacuated Sick.
M2/167934	,,	Norton, T. J.	26, Rodney Street, Oldham Road, Manchester.	25/9/18	26/12/18	,,
DM2/170562	,,	Parsons, P.	Church Lane, Charminster, nr. Dorchester, Dorset.	22/8/16	20/3/19	Demobilised.
MS/4553	,,	†Prickler, A.	9, Wellesley Street, City Road, London, E.C.	21/8/17	22/11/18	Evacuated Sick.
M2/080751	,,	†Phillips, W.	"Homeside," Begelly R.S.O., S. Wales.	21/8/17	14/2/19	Demobilised.
M2/167726	,,	†Parry, W. I.	6, Chelmersford Road, Kirkdale, Liverpool.	22/8/16	24/4/18	Evacuated to Base.
DM2/169245	,,	†Potter, J.	25, Kirby Street, Liverpool.	22/8/16	20/3/19	Transferred to No.6 M.T. Reception Park, Cambrai.
M/298835	,,	†Pow, D. M.	44, Cowgate, Tayfast, Fife.	10/4/18	8/3/19	Transferred to 70 S.B.A.C.
M2/098348	,,	Power, J.	106, Crossley Street, Gorton, Manchester	22/8/16	1919	Eligible for Demobilisation.

† Caterpillar Section.

Regtl. No.	Rank.	Name.	Home Address.	Period of Service with 94 Siege Battery.		Nature of Casualty.
				From	To	
M2/149259	Pte.	Platt, C. W.	8, Cinque Port Square, Rye, Sussex.	15/1/18	1/5/18	Evacuated Sick.
M2/194476	,,	Richardson, W. H.	25, Stourbridge Avenue, Sefton Park, Liverpool.	22/8/16	24/10/18	Transferred to "N" S.A.P. Workshops.
M1/07523	,,	Routledge, W. R.	64, Wellington Road South, Staines Road, Hounslow.	15/1/18	16/12/18	Evacuated to Base.
DM2/180238	,,	†Rumbellow, B.	18, Blagdon Avenue, South Shields.	15/1/18	3/3/19	Evacuated Sick.
M2/194459	,,	Rush, R.	Riddings Farm, Long Town, Cumberland.	22/8/16	21/5/18	Evacuated Wounded.
M2/177996	,,	Smith, H.	60, Queens Road, Hyde Park, Leeds.	22/8/16	2/4/18	Evacuated to Base.
M2/080922	,,	Sharpe, R.	52, Hengoed, Penpedairheol, Pengam, Glamorganshire.	5/1/17	1919	Eligible for Demobilisation.
M/315900	,,	†Smith, A.	23, Cleveleys Road, Upper Clapton, London, N.E.		8/3/19	Transferred to 70 S.B.A.C.

M2/226132	Taylor, A. E.	311, Great Western Street, Rusholme, Manchester.	15/1/18	31/12/18	Demobilised.
M/318503	,,	†Waterson, E. G.	41, Pragell Street, Plaistow, London, E.	10/4/18	1919	Eligible for Demobilisation.
M2/148408	,,	Walton, W. A.	Willow Drove, Newborough, Peterborough.	4/8/18	6/12/18	Evacuated Sick.
M2/052828	,,	Wilkenson, F.	28, Nelson Street, St. Annes-on-the-Sea, Blackpool.	23/8/18	17/11/18	Transferred to 41 S.B.A.C.
M2/10366I	,,	†Young, W. A.	91, Crowther Road, S. Norwood, S.E.	26/8/18	1919	Eligible for Demobilisation.
T4/216256	,,	France, F. J.	44, Bittern Street, Great Suffolk Street, Borough, S.E.	15/1/18	23/5/18	Evacuated Sick.
T4/216226	,,	Smith, A. G.	30, Barlow Street, London, S.E.	15/1/18	17/11/18	Transferred to 327 S.B.A.C.

† Caterpillar Section.

PART VIII.

SUMMARY OF BATTERY POSITIONS OCCUPIED.

(ARRANGED IN CHRONOLOGICAL ORDER.) *

No. of Position as Marked on Map.	Dates Occupied. From	Dates Occupied. To	No. of Guns.	Position.	Location.	Engagements.
						Battles of Somme :
1	7/6/16	22/8/16	4	Bayencourt.	100 yards N. of Church.	Attack on Gommecourt.
2	25/8/16	14/11/16	RX	La Boisselle.	50 yards W. of Site of Church.	Capture of Courcelette, Martinpuich, Le Sars, etc.
3	3/9/16	4/2/17	LX	Ovillers (Spring Gardens).	500 yards S.E. of Village, on By-road connecting Ovillers with Albert-Bapaume Road.	As above, and capture of Thiepval.
	16/11/16	4/2/17	RX			
4	8/2/17	3/3/17	4	Thiepval.	800 yards S.E. of Village, on Thiepval-Pozieres Road.	Capture of Beaumont Hamel, Grandcourt, Miraumont, etc,

No.			RX			
5	4/3/17	18/3/17		Grandcourt.	300 yards S. of Cemetery, on Thiepval-Grandcourt Road.	Capture of Irles.
6	6/4/17	17/5/17	4	Vaulx-Vraucourt.	400 yards S.W. of Sugar Factory (at Cross-roads N.W. of Village), on Beugnâtre-Vaulx-Vraucourt Road.	Attack on Bullecourt, in support of Battle of Arras.
7	24/5/17	9/6/17	4	Dou-Dou Farm (nr. Ploegsteert).	700 yards E. of Romarin Cross-roads	Battle of Messines.
8	10/6/17	18/6/17	4	Le Bizet.	On Canal Bank, 30 yards W. of Ploegsteert-Armentieres Road.	,,
9	1/7/17	13/7/17	3	Nr. Oost Dunkerke.	2,200 yards N.E. of Village, on Oost Dunkerke-Nieuport Bains Road.	Operations on Flanders Coast.
10	14/7/17	2/10/17	4	,,	1,000 yards N.E. of Village on same road as above.	Operations on Flanders Coast.
11	4/10/17	5/12/17	4	,,	1,500 yards E. of Village on S. side of Oost Dunkerke-Nieuport Road.	Operations on Flanders Coast.

* First round fired by No. I Sub-Section, 15/6/16.   Last round fired by No. 4 Sub-Section, 4/11/18.
RX = Right Section.   LX = Left Section.   CX = Centre Section.

No. of Position as Marked on Map.	Dates Occupied. From	To	No. of Guns.	Position.	Location.	Engagements.
12	4/1/18	31/1/18	4	Het Sas (nr. Boesinghe).	100 yards E. of Locks on Yser Canal.	Stationary Warfare subsequent to Passchendaele operations.
13	10/2/18	25/2/18	6	Roisel.	On Southern outskirts of Village; 4 guns on Roisel-Bernes Road, and 2 guns on Roisel-Hancourt Road.	Stationary Warfare prior to March retirement, 1918.
14	27/2/18	21/3/18	LX	Nr. Roisel.	In Cologne Valley, midway between Roisel and Templeux-le-Guérard.	Occupied three weeks prior to, and vacated on, March 21st, 1918.
15	1/3/18	21/3/18	RX	Nr. Hesbécourt.	In Bois Haut, about 500 yards N. of Hesbécourt.	
16	13/3/18	21/3/18	CX	Nr. Hesbécourt.	400 yards S.E. of Hesbécourt, in small quarry.	
17	23/3/18	24/3/18	1	Estrées.	In Village, on N. side of Road.	March, 1918, retreat.

No.						
18	26/3/18	27/3/18	3	Bayonvillers.	On S.W. outskirts of Village, on Bayonvillers - Wiencourt Road.	March, 1918, retreat.
19	27/3/18	28/3/18	3	Villers-Brettonneux.	1,000 yards W. of Village, on N. side of Railway Embankment.	,, ,,
20	28/3/18	14/4/18	1	Petit-Blangy.	300 yards S.E. of Petit-Blangy Cross-roads.	,, ,,
21	30/3/18	2/4/18	2	Bois L'Abbé.	50 yards E. of Chateau in wood, South of Villers-Bretonneux-Amiens Road.	,, ,,
22	30/3/18	14/4/18	1	Petit-Blangy.	800 yards S.E. of Petit-Blangy Cross-roads.	,, ,,
23	3/5/18	24/7/18	LX	Bresle Wood.	Western edge of Wood.	Stationary Warfare, early Summer of 1918.
24	7/5/18	11/7/18	RX	Franvillers.	N.E. outskirts of Village.	
25	9/5/18	19/7/18	CX	Chalk Pit (nr. Ribemont)	1,000 yards N. of Village.	
26	12/7/18	19/7/18	RX	Chalk Pit (nr. Ribemont).	1,000 yards N. of Village.	
	20/7/18	2/8/18	RX became LX	Henencourt.	S.W. outskirts of Village.	

No. of Position as Marked on Map.	Dates Occupied. From	Dates Occupied. To	No. of Guns.	Position.	Location.	Engagements.
27	20/7/18	2/8/18	CX	Baizieux.	Eastern edge of Village.	Stationary Warfare, early Summer of 1918.
28	25/7/18	4/8/18	LX became RX	Nr. Franvillers.	In Valley, 1,500 yards N.E. of Village.	
29	5/8/18	10/8/18	CX	Ribemont.	Eastern end of Village on Main Street.	Initial attacks in final advance.
,,	4/8/18	11/8/18	LX	Ribemont.		
30	6/8/18	24/8/18	RX	Albert Road.	2,000 yards N. of Buire, on S. side of main Albert-Amiens Road.	
31	11/8/18	22/8/18	CX	Ville-sur-Ancre.	30 yards S. of Church.	
,,	12/8/18	29/8/18	LX	Ville-sur-Ancre.	100 yards S. of Church	
32	23/8/18	27/8/18	CX	Dermancourt.	In Village on Main Street, 700 yards W. of Church.	
33	24/8/18	25/8/18	RX	Méaulte.		
34	9/9/18	26/9/18	LX	Villers-Faucon.	W. Bank of Epehy-Roisel Railway, 350 yards S. of Villers-Faucon-St.Emilie Rd	Capture of Epehy, Ronssoy, Templeux-le-Guérard, Hargicourt.

No.	Date	Date	Unit	H.Q.	Position	Operations
34	16/ 9/18	25/ 9/18	RX and CX	Villers-Faucon.	In Valley W. of Village, and 300 yards N. of Longavesnes-St. Emilie Road.	Capture of Epehy, Ronssoy, Templeux-le-Guérard, Hargicourt.
„	10/ 9/18	22/ 9/18				
35	22/ 9/18	27/ 9/18	CX	Villers-Faucon.	W. side of St. Emilie-Roisel Road, 1,000 yards S. of St. Emilie.	
36	25/ 9/18	8/10/18	6	Ronssoy.	On either side of the Epehy-Ronssoy Road, among the extreme W. ruins of Ronssoy.	Capture of Hindenburg Line.
37	29/10/18	4/11/18	Nos. 1, 3, 4 and 6	Bousies.	On the N. side of the track leading N.E. from the Village, and 1,200 yards from its point of departure from the road, Bois de Vendegies - Bousies - Robersart.	Attack cross Canal de la Sambre and capture of Forêt de Mormal.

www.ingramcontent.com/pod-product-compliance
Lightning Source LLC
Chambersburg PA
CBHW030403100426
42812CB00028B/2812/J